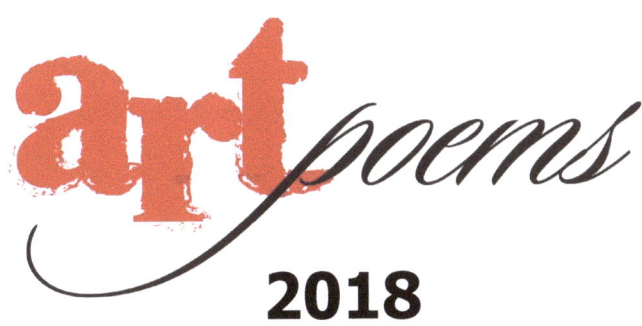

2018

Art and Poems
In Collaboration

Lorraine Walker Williams, Chair
Joseph Pacheco, Vice Chair
Larry Stiles, Secretary, Treasurer

Beth Everhart and Roy Rodriguez, Book Design

ArtPoems, Inc.
www.ArtPoems.org

THE COPYRIGHTS FOR ALL ARTWORK IMAGES AND ALL POEMS ARE RETAINED BY THE ORIGINAL ARTIST AND POET RESPECTIVELY. THE ARTPOEMS NAME AND THE ARTPOEMS LOGO ARE COPYRIGHT © LORRAINE WALKER WILLIAMS. ALL RIGHTS RESERVED.

Love Sees

New poem Inspired by Claude Lyles' painting "Fort Myers Beach"

What do you see?
Do you see the towel, the sand,
the sun?
Do you mind if I ask you to look,
a little deeper?
So again, I ask, "What do you
see?"

I see me!
Yes, this is me!
I am a beautiful mess,
can't you see ?!?!

My pain became my passion
and now I have purpose,
I took my mess
and put it in a message...
Beautiful You Are !

Yes, that's me,
I finally realized
I am Enough !

the little girl
who wrote in her journal
to hide ~~her pain~~
never thought
she was beautiful
enough, stands
before you asking
you to take another look,
"What do you see?"

her hope is that you see me,
but not just me, she hopes
you see the beautiful light
that shines brightly
throughout this beautiful
mess-
enger
Love sees you and me.

~ Jamilla D. Brooks

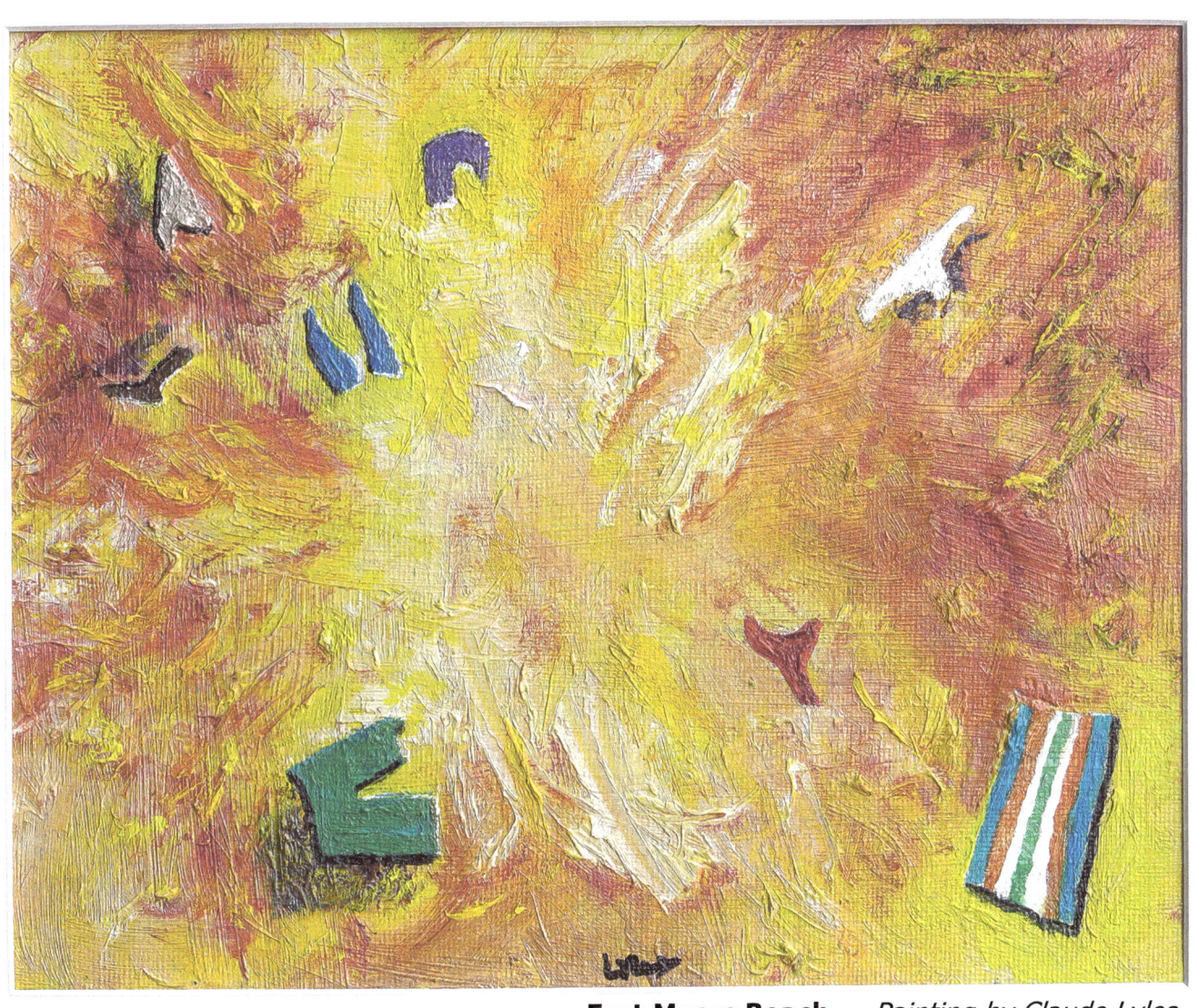

Fort Myers Beach - *Painting by Claude Lyles*

Thought Of The Day...

Provided Inspiration for artist Paul David Adamick's new mixed-media "A Land Of Peace"

EVERY GOOD AND PERFECT GIFT IS FROM ABOVE.
JAMES 1:17 (NIV)

Give me the courage to share my spoken words among your people,
let these words vibrate their eardrums rockin' BEATS like I'm Dr. Dre
not quite a doctor yet, but one day I will head in that direction.
There is only one direction and that is up,
when I am down, I look up, when I am up I look up,
up, up, and never away!

Keep my gaze towards you always and forever
I want to spend days dazed by your beauty
I don't have to see you to know that you are there,
no, not there or there but you are right here rockin' the mic with me
granting me the courage I asked for in the beginning.
Hear me Roar, like the lion from the *Wizard of Oz*.
There is no black magic, just a vail
can't you tell

I am a new person, oh since you probably can't see it then you won't believe it.
But if you put your hand on your chest and feel the vibrations with every beat,
you breathe new life, every moment is a moment to heart the world,
let me correct myself, every moment is a moment to share your heart with the world.
The heart is liking life, rockin' to the beat so you don't stop the music
let it flow in you and through you
because the only one who checks for you is Him, but do you check for Him?
Can you say you seek Him?
Can you say that you trust Him?
Can you say that you Believe?

Now when you say that you believe, ask yourself do I truly believe
that He took lashes and nails for you and me?
Would you lay down your life for a friend? stranger? lover? family?
Well we all are one who came from the Great One, the King of Kings.
If life skips off beat place your hands on your heart and just listen...
You have the Best DJ right here...
Jesus to the rescue!

~ Jamilla D. Brooks

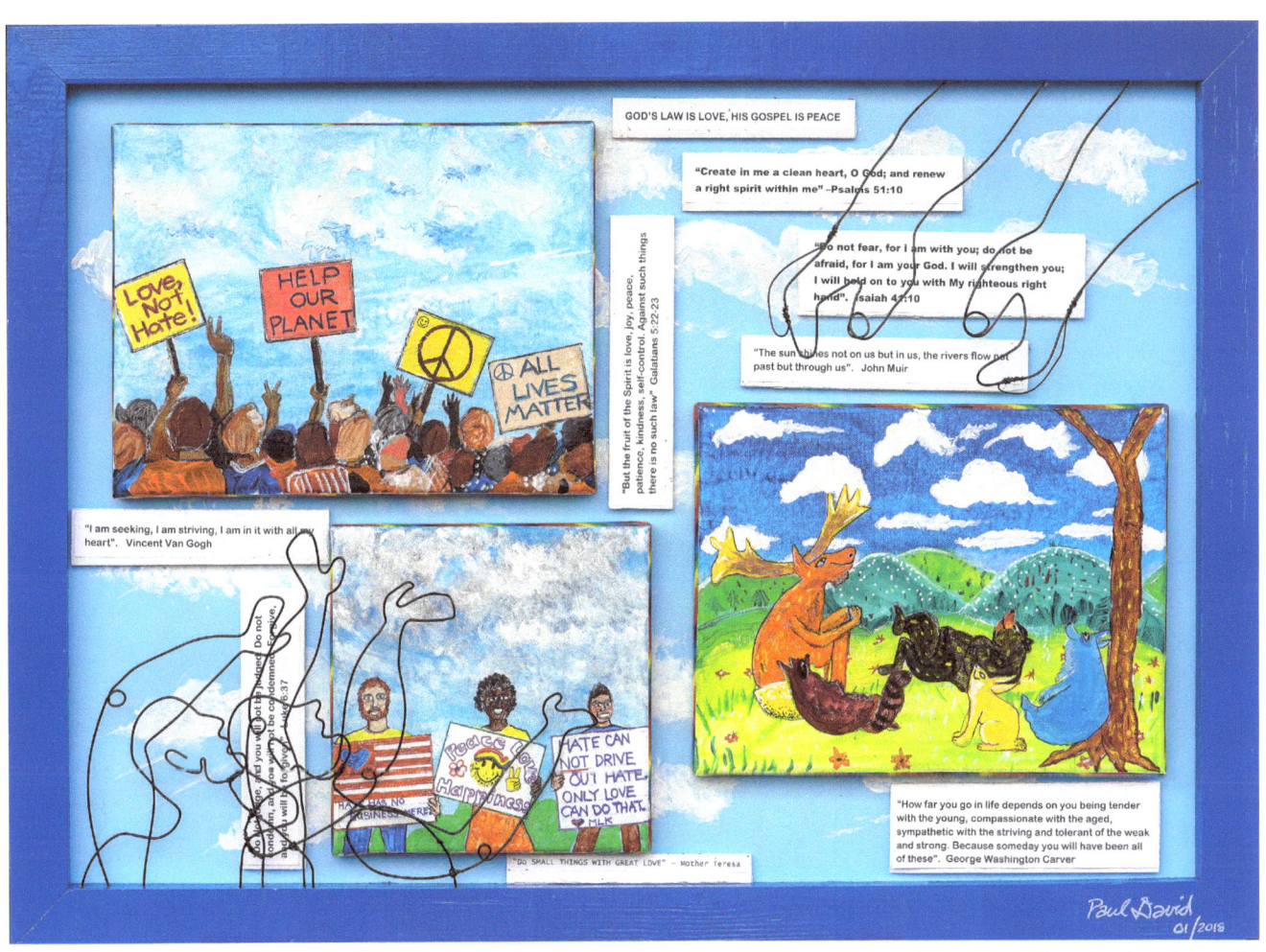

A Land of Peace—*New mixed media by Paul David Adamick*

Shadow Rays

New poem Inspired by Lesley Morrow's painting "Orchid"

> THE ORCHID GROWS WHERE OTHERS CANNOT, ENDURING HARDSHIPS OF HUNGER AND THIRST, AND IS ONLY LOOSELY TIED TO THE THINGS THAT SUPPORT IT"
>
> CONFUCIUS

She was sure it died, bare
stick in crusted glass bowl, dried
silhouette screamed before grime
of winter on her kitchen window, until
one trivial bud on the spindly stalk

emerged out of demise, tinged
by myriad hues to glow, white
flame and shade, joined in time
with other tiny blossoms lined
up free style dancers, perfume

climbing over stale coffee, yesterday's
dishes, piled for the time clouds creeping
from her brain's back corners can be blown
by breeze her gray, dread wide-awake
nightmares will never let return.

She feels shadows lean against skin
admitted into her chest, purple and gray
current, deep red in blood, caressing
its path in sinew and bone. She drinks
in steam as scalding water
fills the sink.

~ Dan Reed England

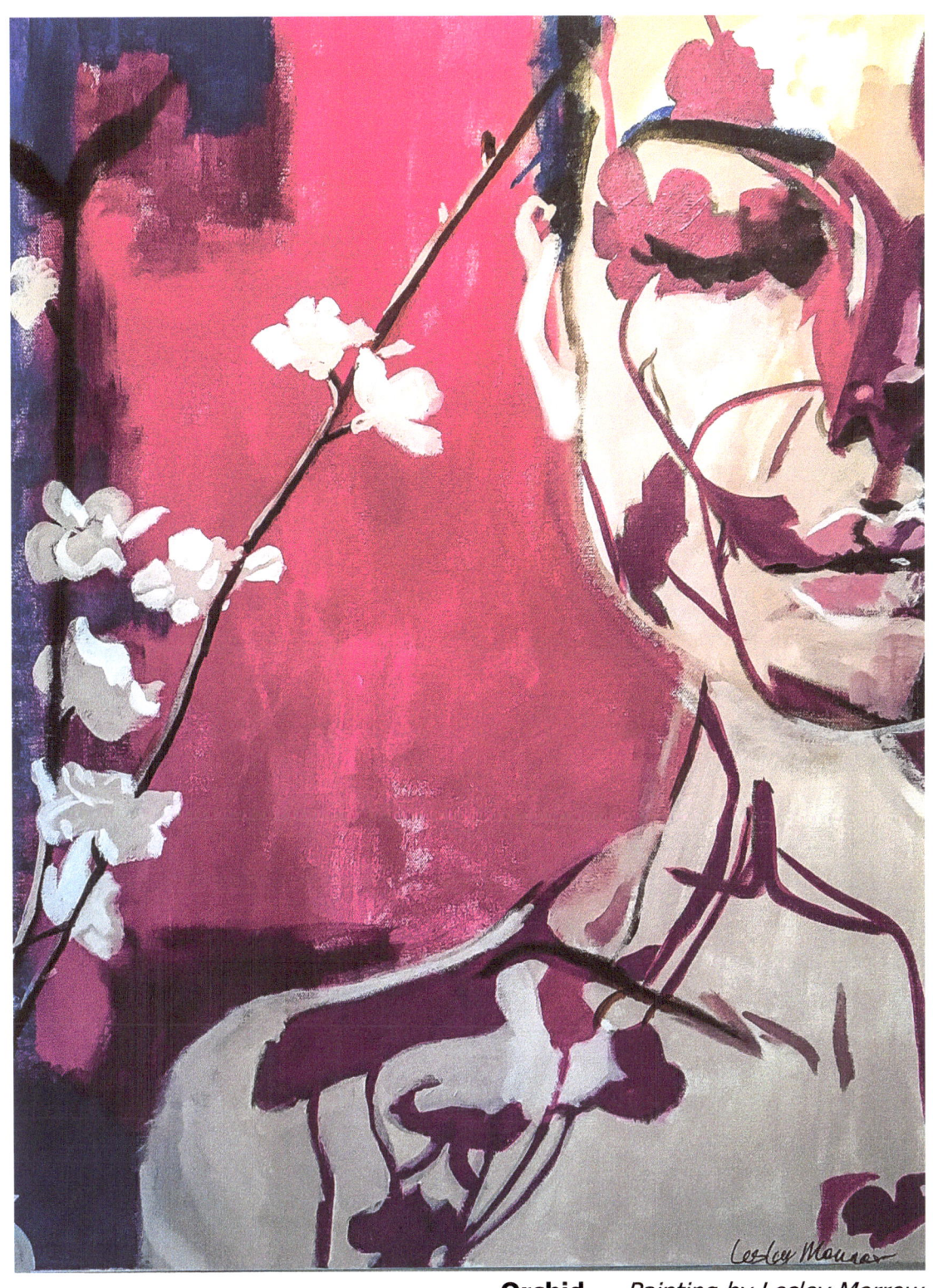

Orchid - *Painting by Lesley Morrow*

Wilding

Provided Inspiration for artist Scott Guelcher's new painting "Wilding Memories"

Swinging on a fence
drunk on the grand ecstasy
Head thrown back laughing
drunk on splendors of being
glorious nine year old boys

Zooming from one laugh
to another, back again
Cartwheels, back flips, jumps
Pirates fencing with sticks
Beautiful laughter, pure glee

Brown forms lithe, limber
Uproars blasted in Patois
shouts for sheer pleasure
shouts over wild and frantic
barking from one boy's mongrel

The dog back and forth
tail semaphores his mad glee
He must find the place
the place with the greatest fun
That Illusion moving always

Dusk glows, unwelcomed
Mothers arrive in housecoats
greeting their neighbors
Calling home their warriors
shouting down cries of protest

Please, it's not dark
We need just ten minutes more
just five minutes more
I promise I'll do my homework
I'll even wash the dishes

Just five minutes more
Five more minutes of freedom
Five minutes to run
climb, chase, laugh, roll on the ground
Drunk on being a nine year old boy

~ Dan Reed England

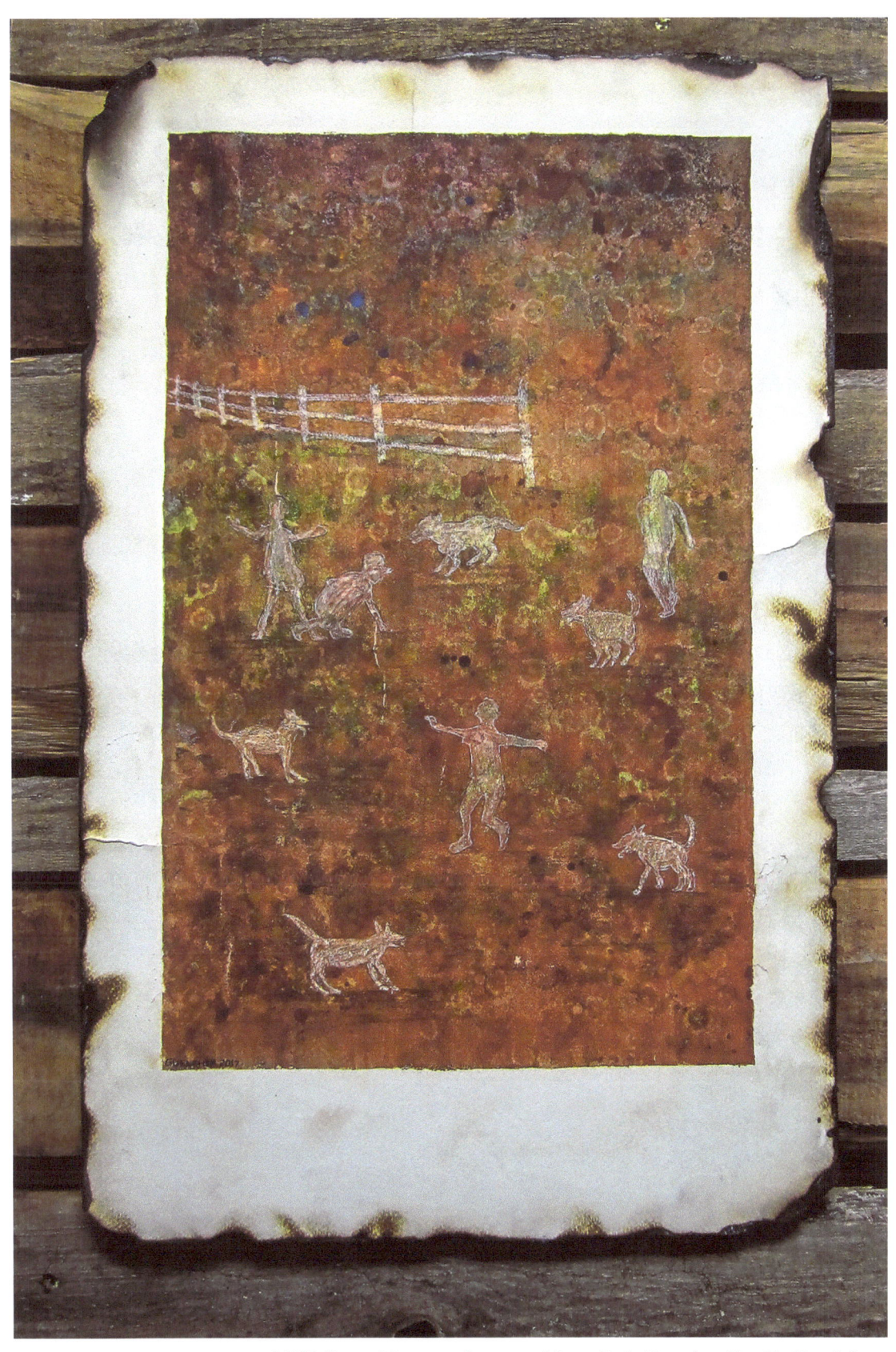

Wilding Memories - *New Painting by Scott Guelcher*

The Last Woman on Earth Works Her Magic

New poem Inspired by Lawrence Massing's photograph "Circadian Rhythm Continuum"

The scent of rain
hangs heavy
on this empty
smoldering sphere.
Silence fills the air;
it echoes memories
of what had been,
of what is lost.
A mournful moon
hovers,
waits, watches.

Now is the time.
The rain falls like tears
relieved of grief.
I wander and search
for clues.

From my gris gris bag
I toss my alchemy
on ashy sand.
Dead brush
    Brown twigs
    Dry leaf
detritus of war:
    A sign
    A circle
on Earth vanquished by man.

Ghosts of life leave designs:
A continuum
    A sign
    A circle

Like a golden halo
the sun, a blazing orb
rises.
Hope emerges
From my bag of magic.

~ Joyce Berrian Ferrari

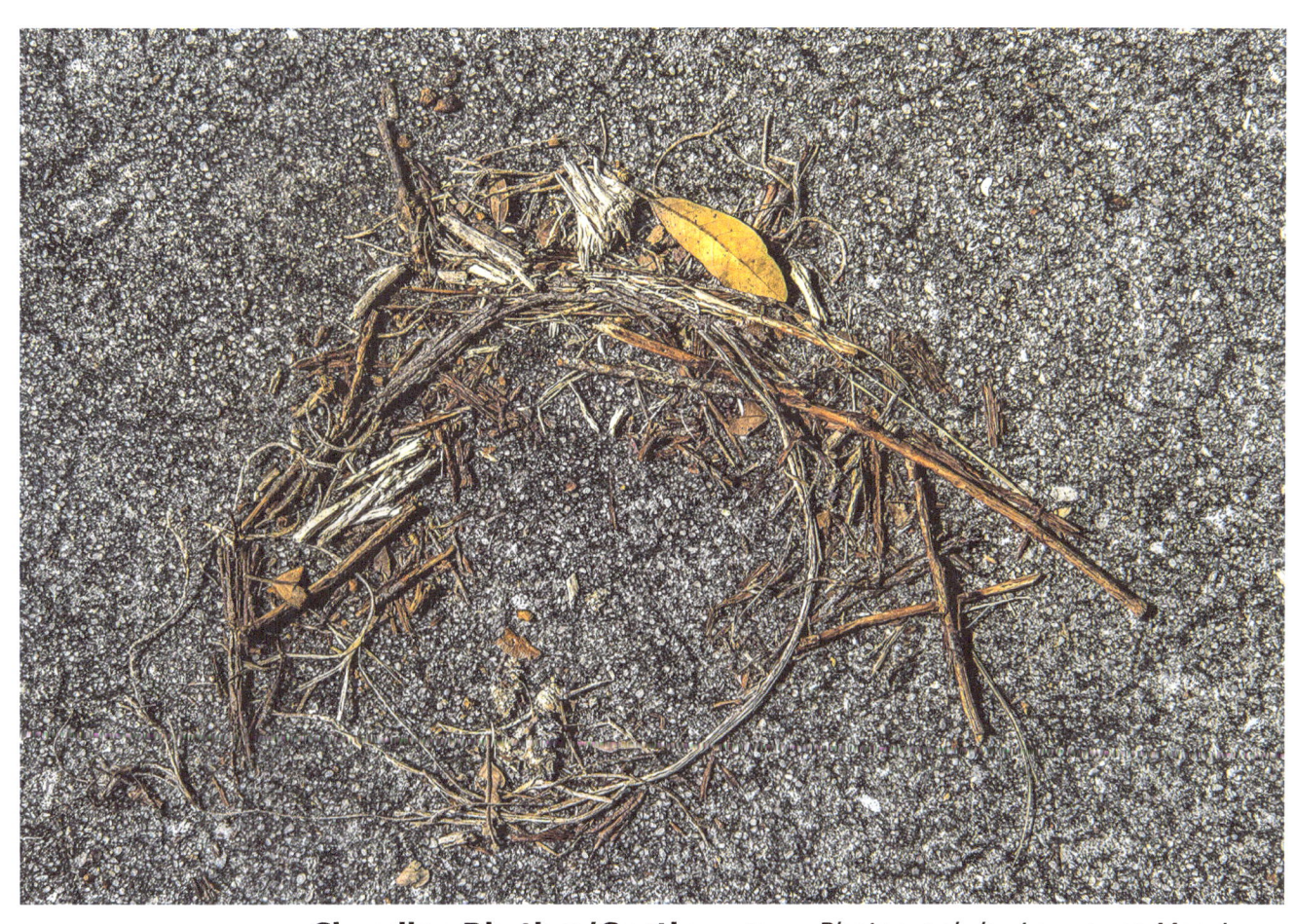

Circadian Rhythm/Continuum - *Photograph by Lawrence Massing*

Snapshot

Provided Inspiration for artist Barbara Gage Mulford's new painting "Snapshot"

Rummaging through
old photographs
black and white
grainy with age
I find myself
running through a field
dried-out hay crunching
under my stocking- covered feet
the only clothing
on my lithe limber body
I catch my breath
longing to be back
far away in that moment
long dark hair floating
around me a feather
tucked behind one ear
I am captured
in a country summer breeze
our clothing lay scattered
in the open field
the scent of new mown hay lingering
on my skin still wet from rapture

He is not in the picture
photographer   voyeur   lover
of fleeting moments
the prickly grass is not visible
only me clutching
a bouquet of daisies
me fleeing in wild abandonment

~ Joyce Berrian Ferrari

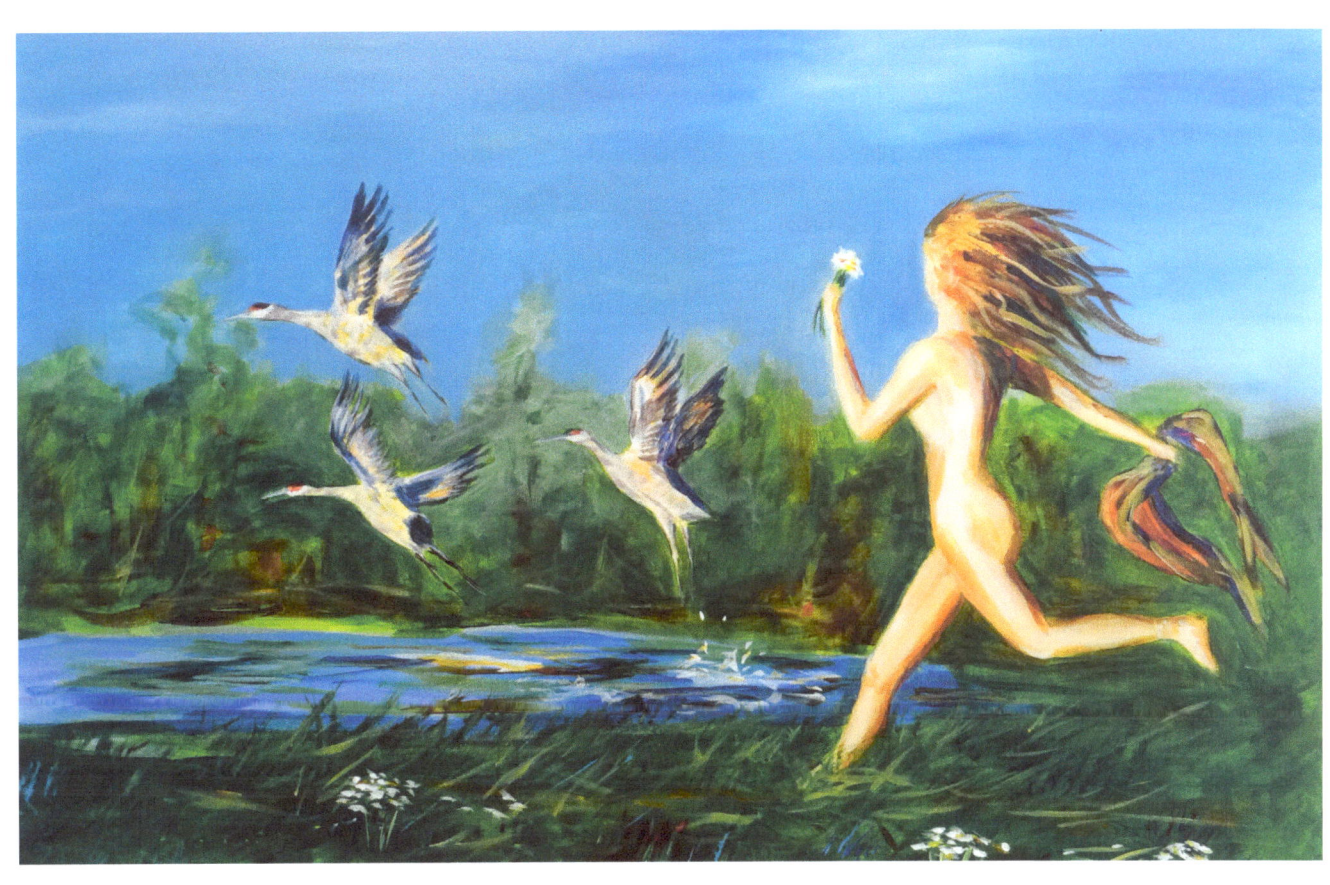

Snapshot - *New Painting by Barbara Gage Mulford*

Perspectives

New poem Inspired by Roy Rodriguez's photograph "Frond With Bug: OK, So It's Not A Bug"

1.

Come. Look at me.

I am debris, after storm,

on an island, ravaged and worn,

eyeless, earless, disconnected,

frayed like useless wire.

Still I gasp; I struggle to escape,

captive in this heap of disaster;

desperate for a path to that

remembered bright sky,

a reminder of what once was:

one lonely scrap of hope.

2.

Come. Imagine me:

I am bug alive,

my arm, one leg, fringed,

already free,

loosed ligaments climbing

this slender stairway,

ready to leap to pure light.

I am a single joyful note

on some musician's symphonic staff,

rising, aching to sing

into the crescendo of frond and sky:

the pure azure of delight.

~ Christine Godwin

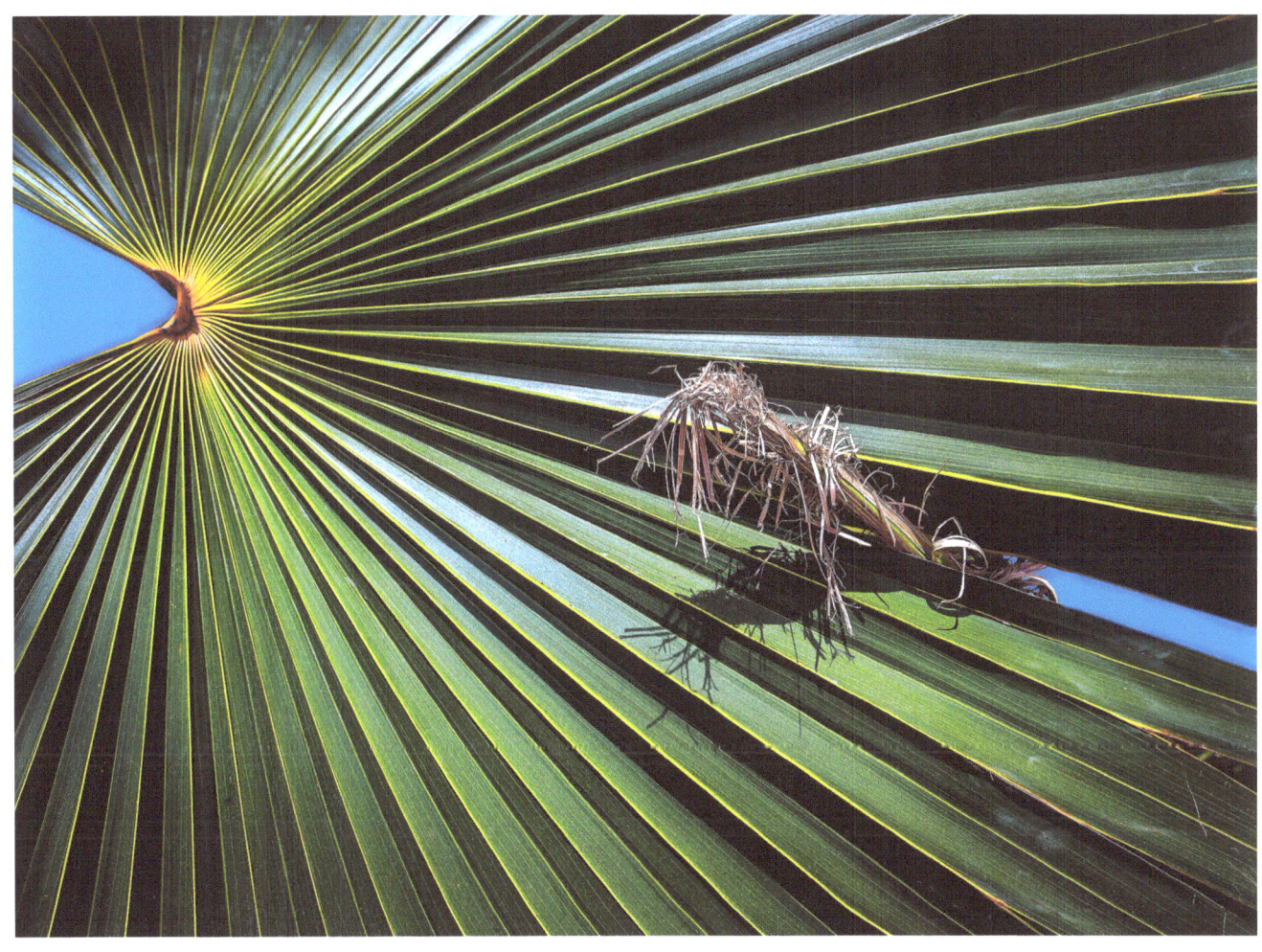

Frond With Bug: OK, So it's Not A Bug - *Photograph by Roy E. Rodriguez*

In The Caves of Chauvet

Provided Inspiration for artist Honey Costa's new artwork "The First Artist"

The **Chauvet-Pont-d'Arc Cave** in the Ardèche department of southern France is a cave that contains some of the best-preserved cave paintings in the world dating between 37,000 and 28,000 years ago.

Deep inside him
story swells
struggling so fiercely
to find its way
through the knots and loops
of his wakening brain.

In these indigo caves
and flickering flames,
his fingers blindly meet
the cool clean
Chauvet walls.

Something he needs to do-
there is no name for it yet,
no alphabet or words.
So he dips down into
the smeared blood and mustard
flower mash,
places a tentative finger,
curves a fine line;

remembers the wild buffalo
and boar of yesterday's hunt;
adds haunches, tail,
splintery hooves,

and there it is:
his memory,
his first story,

himself.

~ Christine Godwin

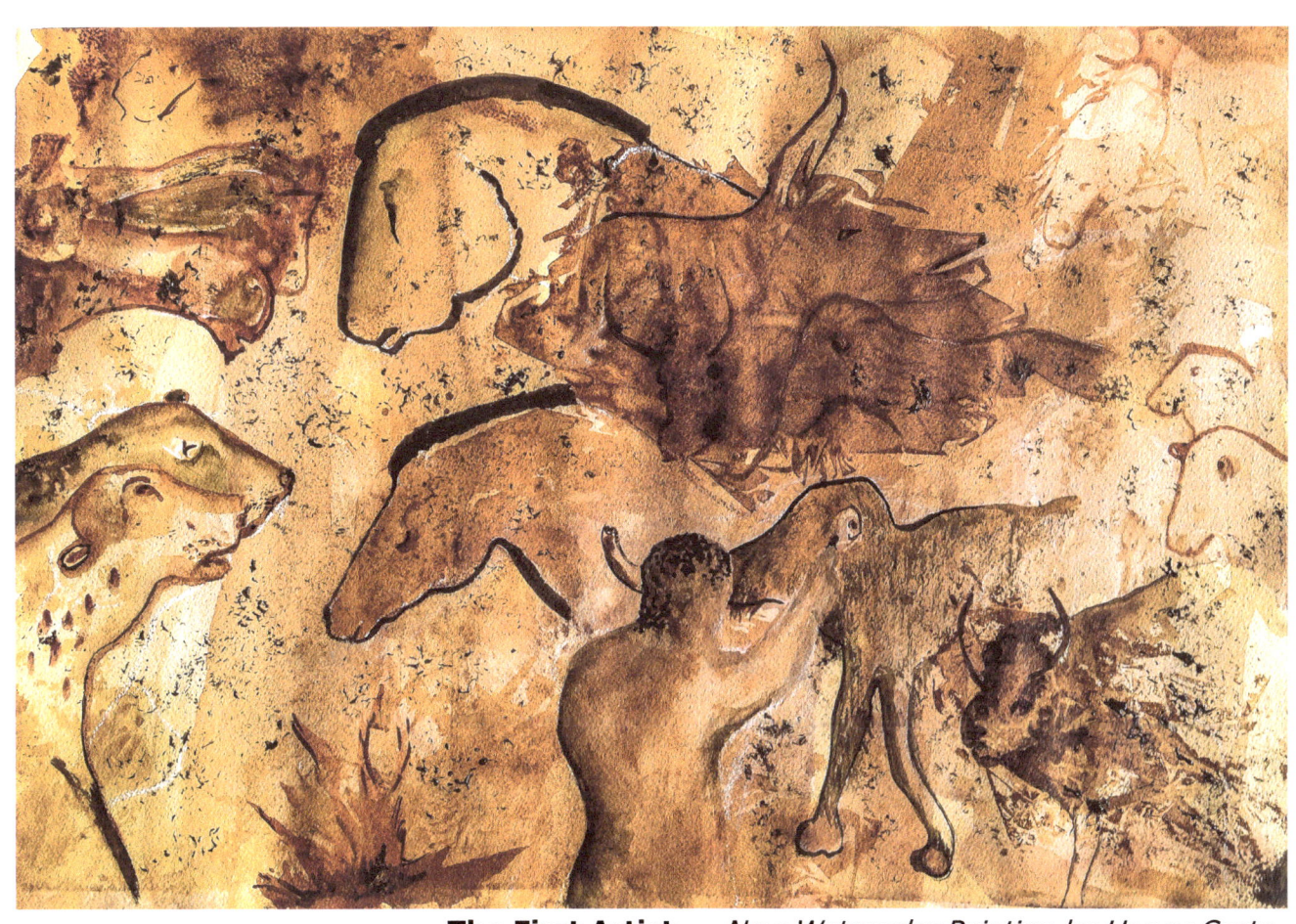

The First Artist - *New Watercolor Painting by Honey Costa*

In the Garden of Eden

New Poem Inspired by Paul David Adamick's mixed-media "Oh No, You Know What's Next!"

I've often wondered, was it boredom
Made Eve pluck that forbidden treat?
Telling Adam, oh so coyly,
"Try it, darling, it's so sweet!"
When the serpent slithered up to her
And suggested she should eat.
The fruit would grant them knowledge,
The reptile did insist,
This possibility appealed so much,
She simply couldn't resist.

In their garden, it was perfect,
Nothing unpleasant there,
No contention or pollution,
Just peace and fragrant balmy air.
An array of all of nature
Laid out at their feet,
Theirs to pick and choose from,
Their life was quite complete.

Perhaps God in all His wisdom
Forgot to delete one flaw
From His new creation
For it does affect us all.
We share a love of power,
And it certainly does seem true,
Adam and Eve's choice to disobey
Destroyed their paradise for two.

So the next time you encounter someone,
Urging you to "Try this, please!"
Remember what happened to Adam
When he took the advice of Eve.

~ Sandy Greco

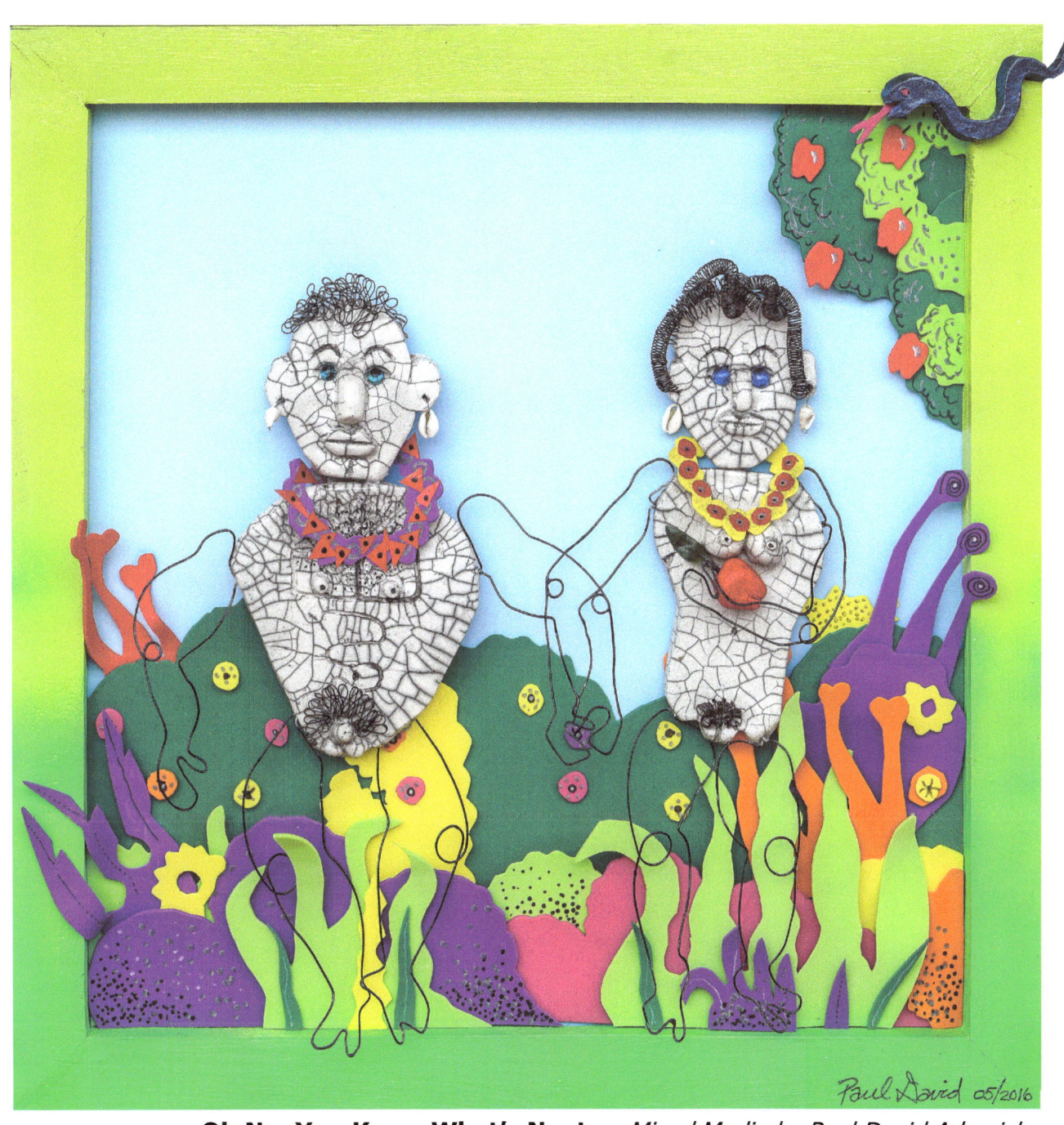

Oh No, You Know What's Next - *Mixed Media by Paul David Adamick*

Currents

Provided Inspiration for artist Lawrence Massing's new photograph "Untitled"

I longed to love you
Always
With that same intensity
To feed the fire of my desire,
It could not be.

Just as a moth that flies too closely
To the flame must surely die,
So too, I,
Could not exist
Apart from you.

For then, I breathed your very air,
Synchronized my every breath
As we slept
Entwined.
To climb inside your mind
And become a part of you,
Was all that I desired.

Time's subtle changes cause a shift,
Familiarity breeds complacency
Comfort replaces intensity
Love remains
But those raging rivers have been crossed
Our younger selves now changed or lost.

Both disappointed and relieved,
I did believe
Only calm waters lay ahead
Not understanding
I am sailing on a different sea.

~ Sandy Greco

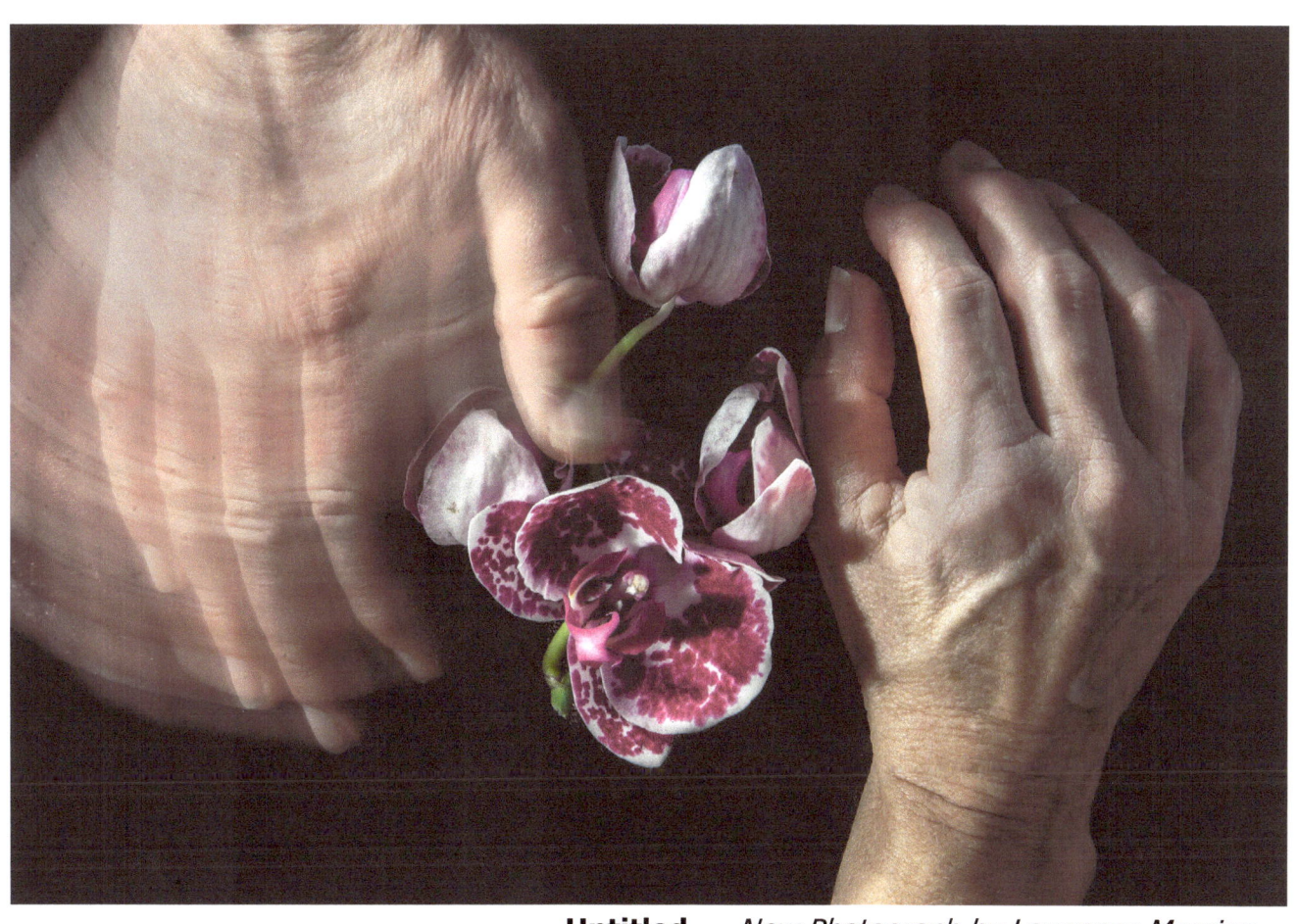

Untitled - *New Photograph by Lawrence Massing*

Pink

New Poem Inspired by Honey Costa's painting "Coastal Habitat"

Here flamingos stand
in the brilliant blue Gulf waters
that lap the golden sands
of a thousand islands.
Here flamingos gather, each balanced
on one pencil-thin backward-bent leg,
black beaks curved down
to scoop up tiny brine shrimp.
With age their feathers change
from gray at birth
to pink, even orange and red,
while they eat
more and more pink shrimp.
Some hide from view
in the quiet green shadows
of Caloosahatchee oxbows.
Others slowly strut, flaunt their color
while they preen and feast together
in the sun.
A gathering is called by some
a colony, a stand, or a regiment
but I love best their festive designation:
    a flamboyance of flamingos.

~ Mary Beth Lundgren

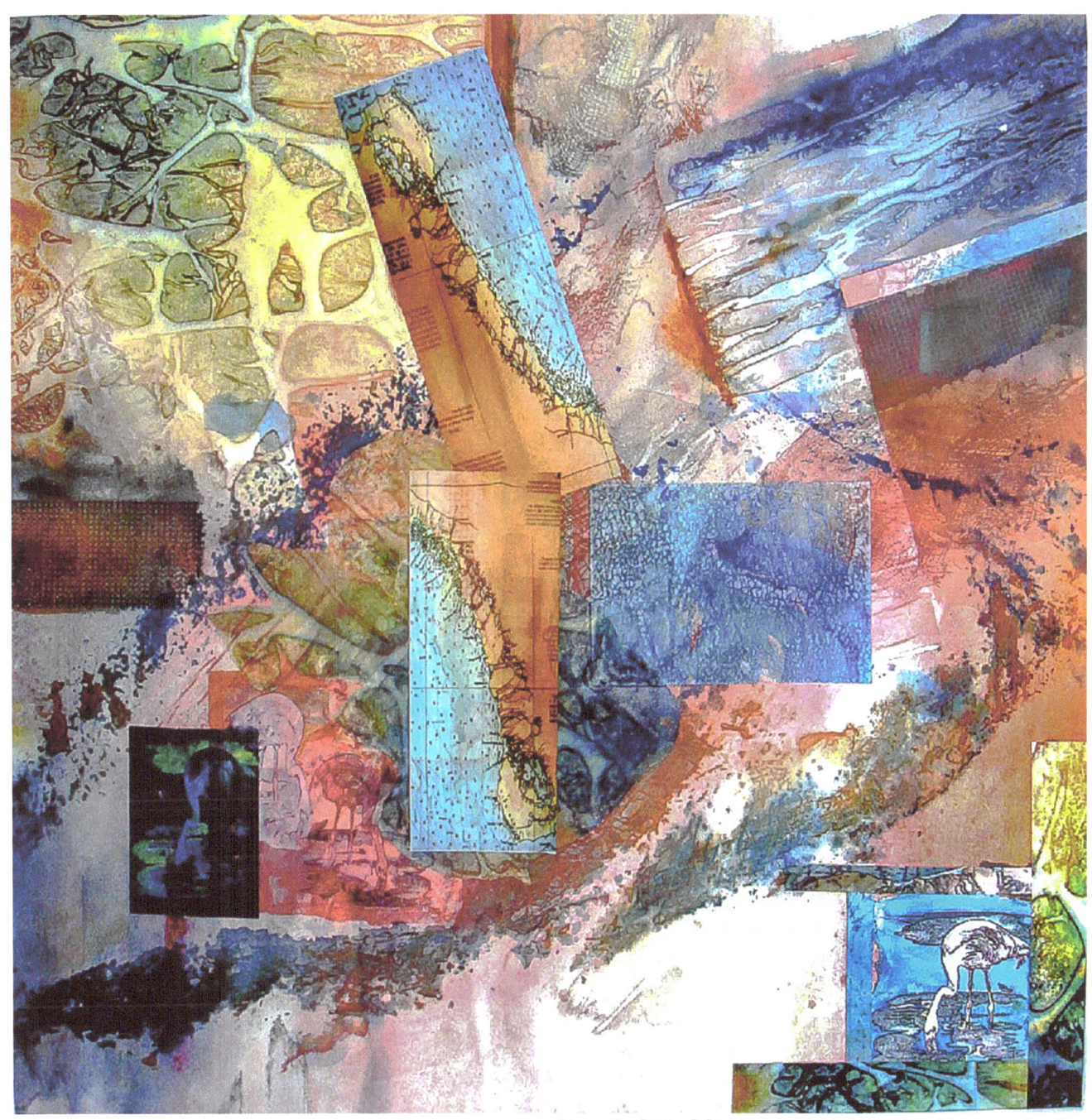

Coastal Habitat - *Painting by Honey Costa*

Roses At The Range

Provided Inspiration for artist Lesley Morrow's new Painting "Soldiers Falling"

A POEM OF WITNESS ….FOR THOSE WHO COME HOME BROKEN AND THOSE WHO TRY TO HELP.

In gorgeous Texas weather he shoots
for an hour then pauses,
admires red roses round the perimeter—
same as those his wife planted at home

while he was gone for a third tour.
They're happy, these roses, dancing—
and he dances too till his buddies stare
at him, each other, him again.

Back to freaking Iraq?

Color deepens as the roses dance,
advance toward him,
redder and redder, *too* red
as if bleeding, falling, and he

No! I won't go!

slams in a magazine as they aim
at him and he shoots first—
one shot, one down, then the other—
empties the magazine,

and red roses burst into bloom
on their chests.

~ Mary Beth Lundgren

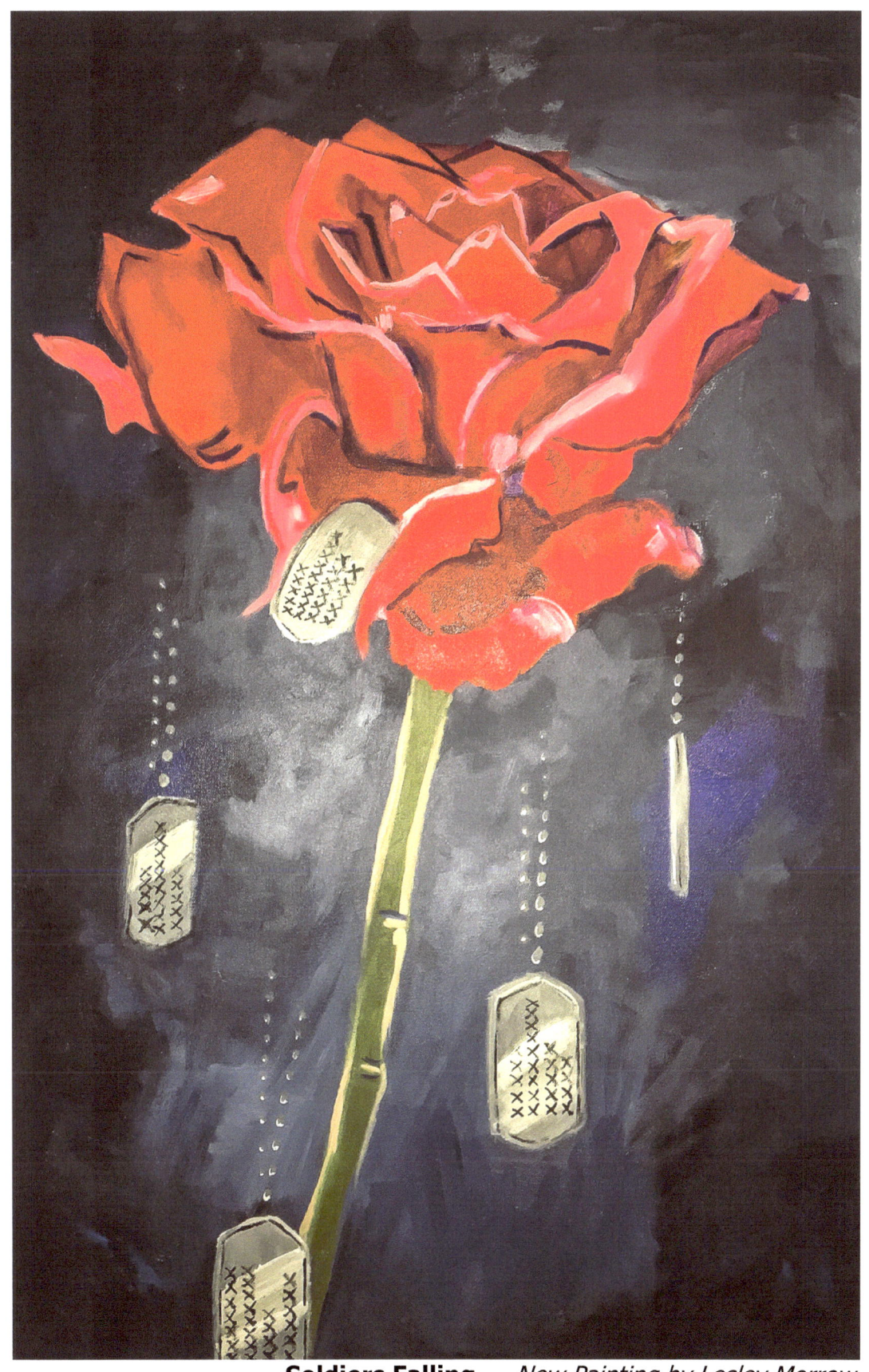

Soldiers Falling - *New Painting by Lesley Morrow*

Paddling with Dolphins: A Story Poem

New poem Inspired by Buck Ward's photograph "Paddling with Dolphins"

Grandma falls.
Walking across our living room, she takes a tumble.
I watch for concussion, bruises—

Nothing broken but her confidence.
Her spirits lag like canoes under the eaves.
I decide the only cure for this is kayaking.

Rising in pre-dawn, I wake her.
In the morning mist, we hook boats to bicycles,
Pedal to the Sound, twin ships bobbing in our wake.

We set off in cool air and warm water,
Trust our senses to guide us,
Sloshing waves and dripping paddles our companions.

Slowly, surely, we flow through the brine,
Breathe in tandem as we work toward wholeness—
Our sole destination.

Grandma gasps, loud, and I startle.
Turning about, I see her, safe behind me,
Awash in the golden peach of dawn—

Paddling with dolphins.

~ Holly L. McEntyre

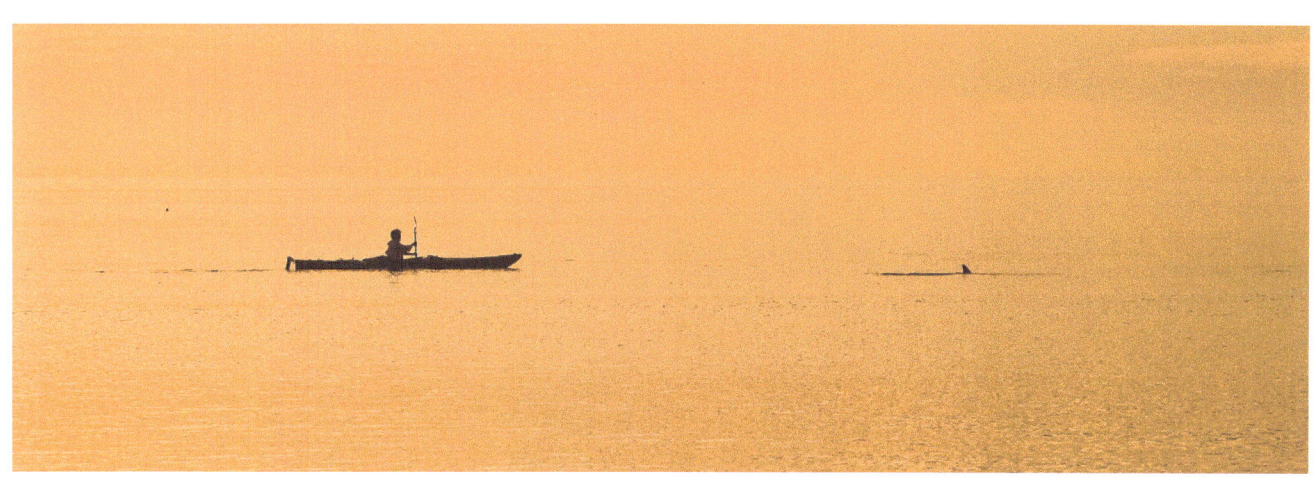

Paddling With Dolphins - *Photograph by Buck Ward*

After My Evening Meal

Provided Inspiration for artist Claude Lyles' new pastel painting "Sanibel After Dinner"

After my evening meal
    I wander the garden,
    leaf through palm fronds,
    promenade past bromeliads.

Slow my pulse to the pace
    of this world,
    drops form and fall,
    frogs chirrup in the cooling air.

Feel the soles of my feet
    on dewy ground,
    kiss of sunset on my crown,
    inhale the incense of life.

See the first star
    unmask its grace,
    shine across light years
    to this perfect place.

~ Holly L. McEntyre

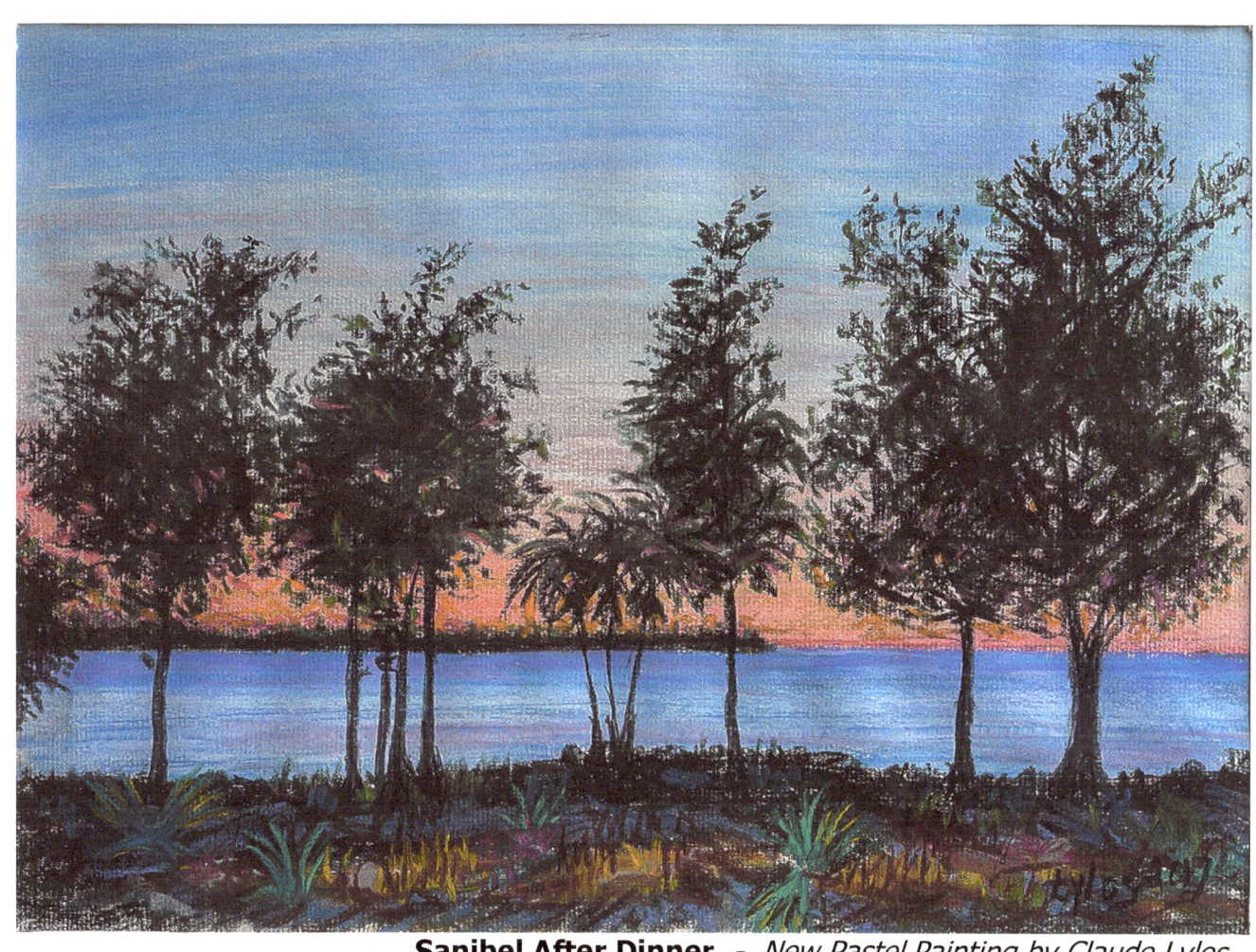

Sanibel After Dinner - *New Pastel Painting by Claude Lyles*

Truckin' to Eternity

New poem Inspired by Beverly Taht's painting "Travelin' "

I'm not givin' up, you gave up on me
Toyota, Ford, Dodge and the new Chevy
Though their new models eclipse me
My desires drive on

Botox the gaps in my grinning grill
Grease my bearings, align my wheels,
Sand my dimples to shining sheen
Gap the plugs, inflate the tires, fuel my marbled machine

Pick-up truckers crave old but new
I'll be an antique two years in June,
Good for collectors, historians of trends
But I know what you know, the fickleness of trends

Memories go dark, sentiments dull
I strain to remember my showroom spell
I trucked your load
You drove me like Hell

Bein' a truck is like bein' a toad
Follow the leader, far down the road
Turn to look back, your story's done told
You're just a trade-in, new truck's been sold

~ Gary McLouth

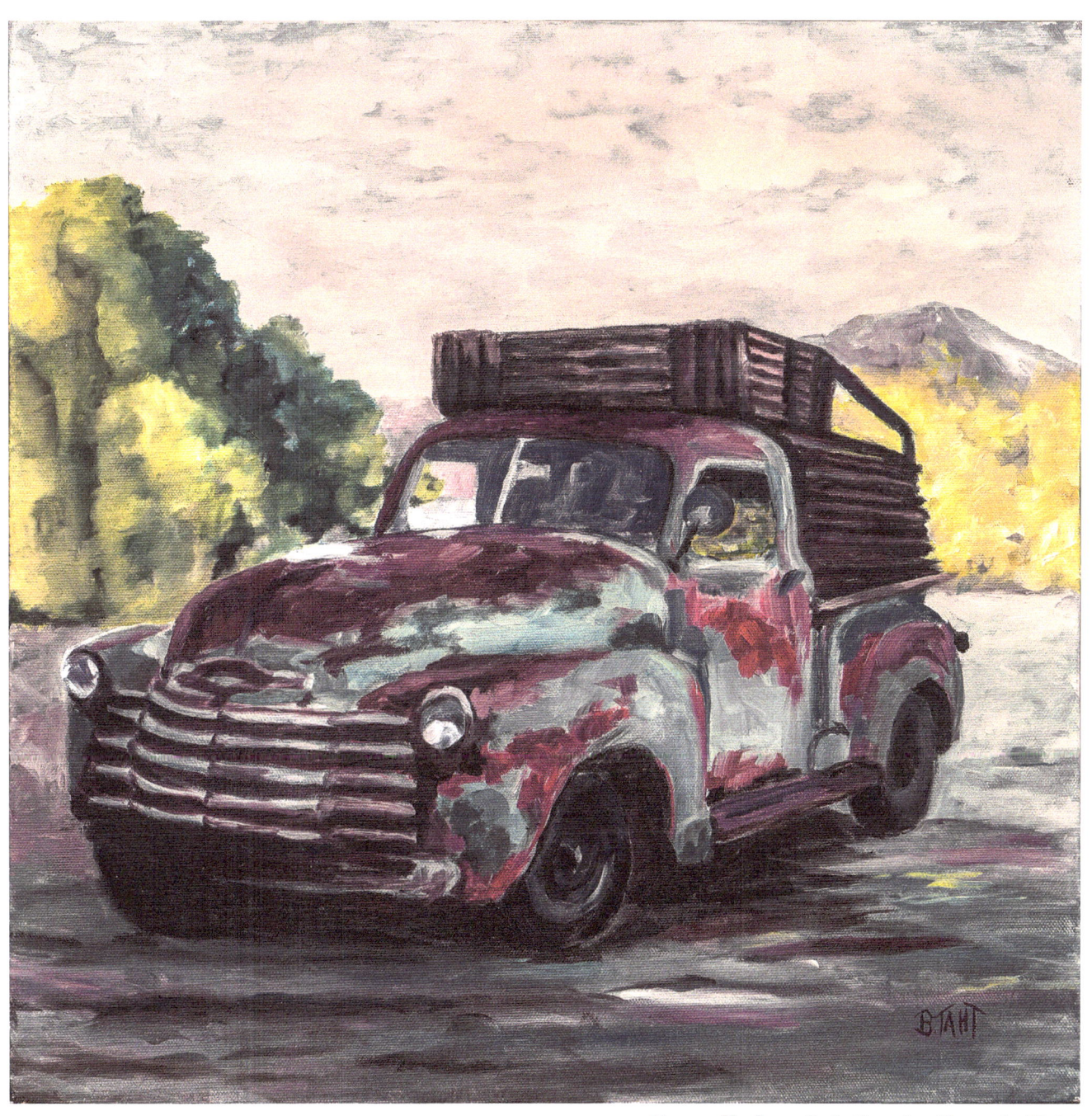

Travelin' - *Painting by Beverly Taht*

Good Work

Provided Inspiration for artist Buck Ward's new photograph "Kindling Spirits"

Poetry doesn't pay much, does it?
The woodsman sighs to me
As he pulls the axe blade from
A near split piece of cedar
And cuts another arc over his head
Like an Indian laboring over a log
He is digging out
And lets it slice the air silver
Straight through the cedar's crack
To the chopping block

How much you gettin' for splitting the wood
I ask
He lays the axe on the block
Steps into the September woods
That overhang the shed

A man pissing outdoors
Draws companionship
I step in and find a mossy rock to aim at

The maples are flaming, oaks
Just beginning to turn
A solitary red and yellow tipped leaf
Meanders to the ground

Not enough he says
But it's good work
And I can piss anywhere I want to
Any time

~ Gary McLouth

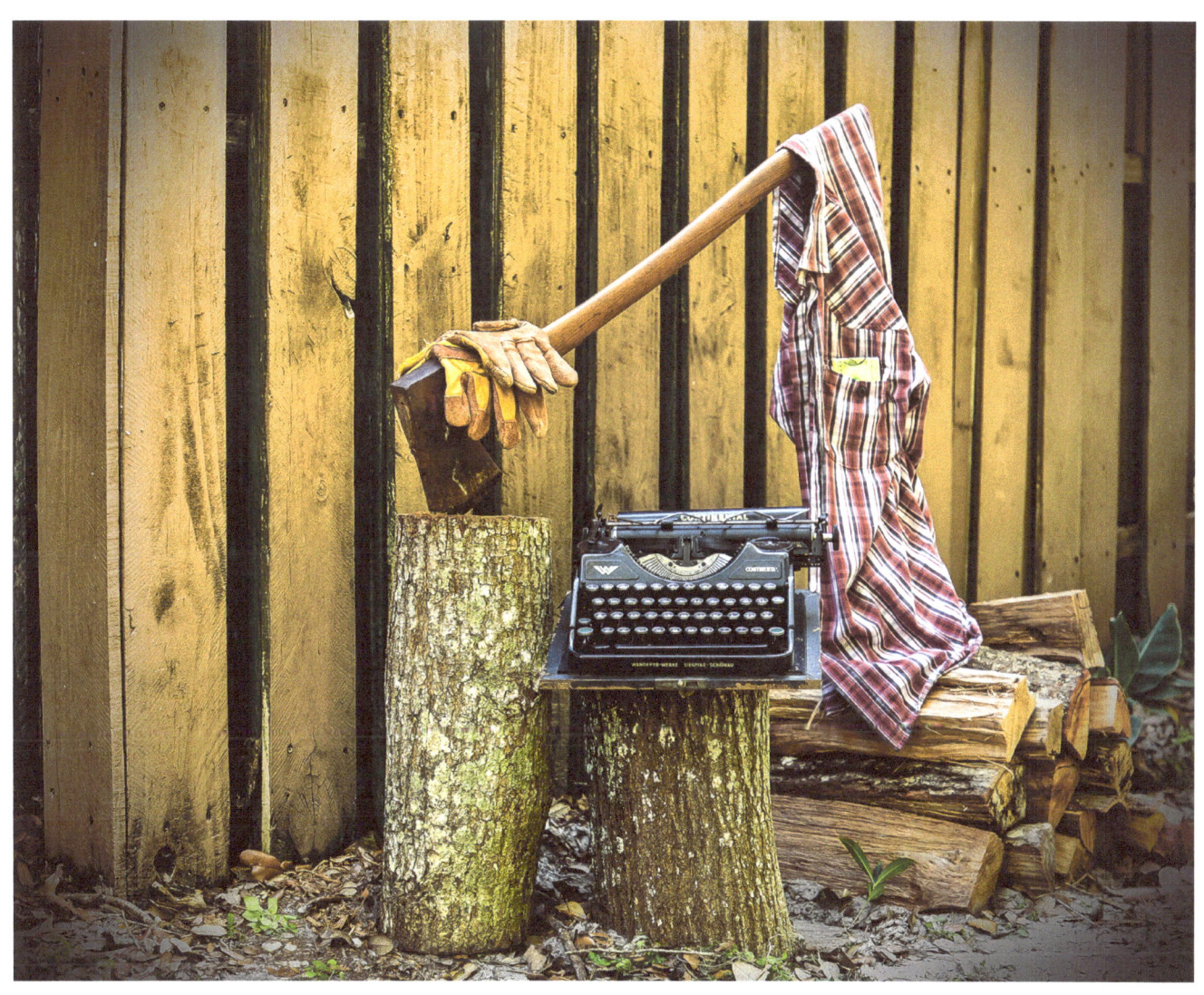

Kindling Spirits - *New Photograph by Buck Ward*

Continuum

New Poem Inspired by William Kramer's painting "Mother and Child"

As a seed in the womb, my heartbeat was yours.
The key to me flowed through our shared cord.
When my life spilt out from you, I held on tight.
I suckled at your breast, made your body my bed.
I tugged on you till lifted in arms that never tired.

As an adult, those arms opened, set me free,
to imprint my own DNA on the universe. My
life mimicked its spirals, circles, chaos & calm.
I fell into black holes. Bore a cross of sorrows.
I rose in a confetti of light. Wore a crown of stars.

As a senior, I began to slow down, to slide inward.
Pieces of me aged into my faded memories of you.
Skin thinned into liver spots traced from your body.
Hair whitened into your curly cap of lambswool.
When I drew my last breath, we were one again.

~ Marilyn Mecca

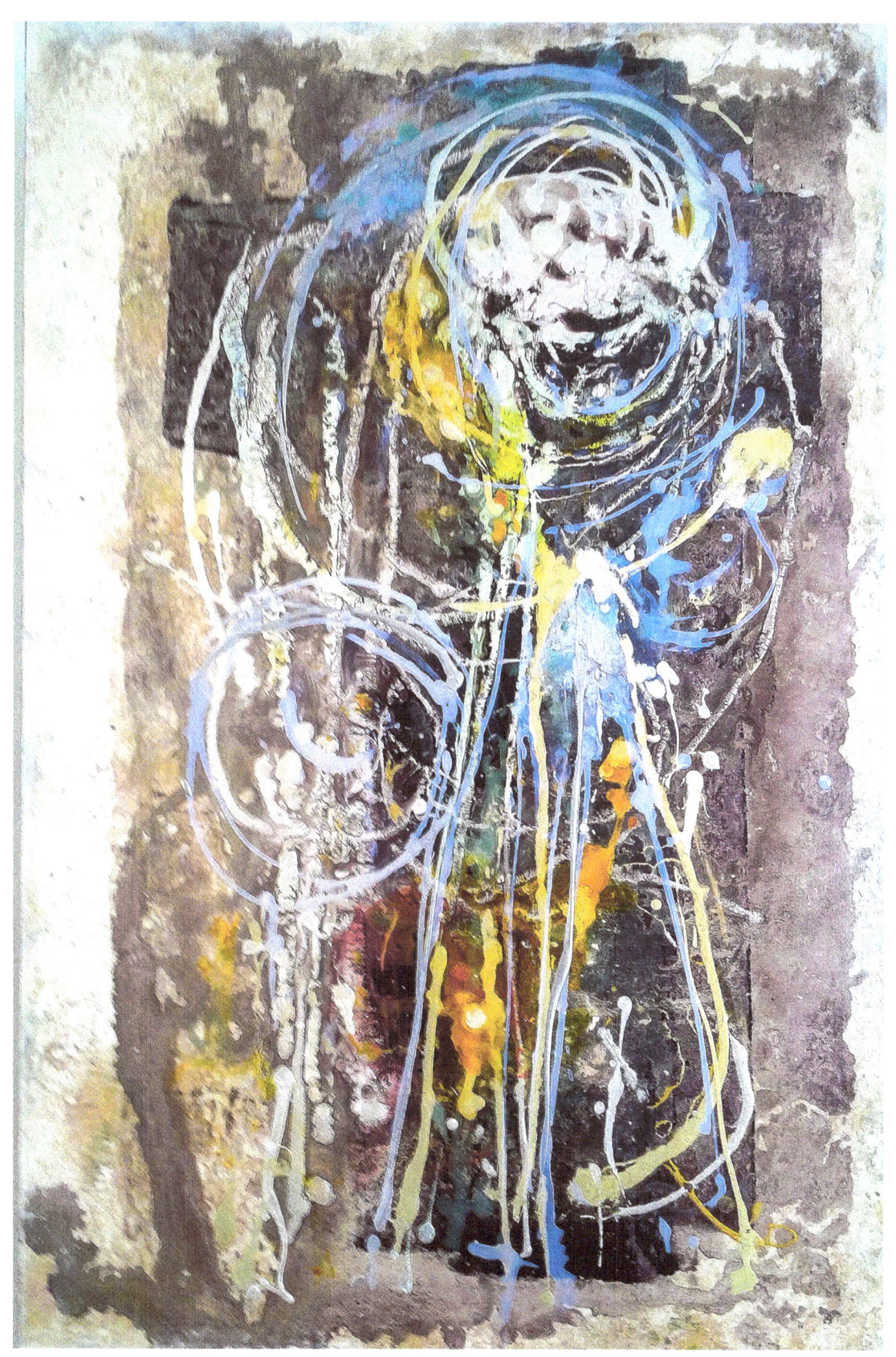

Mother and Child - *Abstract Painting by William Kramer*

Boat Basin Blues

Provided Inspiration for Artist Roy Rodriguez's New Photograph "When Life is Only Memories"

His torso forms an apostrophe,
an inconspicuous human curl,
hunched deep into himself,
hidden from the $20 burger crowd
at the 79th Street Boat Basin.

A breeze off the Hudson River
cools his weather-lined face.
Smudges of New Jersey fill
his vision and his empty time.
There is nowhere for him to go.

People on the promenade pass,
purposely oblivious, skirting
his body and his odors, denying
his existence. There is no space
where he does not offend.

What erased him, made his life
slide inwards, then dissolve?
Did he once ride a limo to his
wedding and a bright future?
Play stickball with a son?

From a park bench, close enough
to see, yet not be seen, I study him
as a work of art, a flawed statue
that fate sculpted with the wrong
mix of dreams and disappointments.

~ Marilyn Mecca

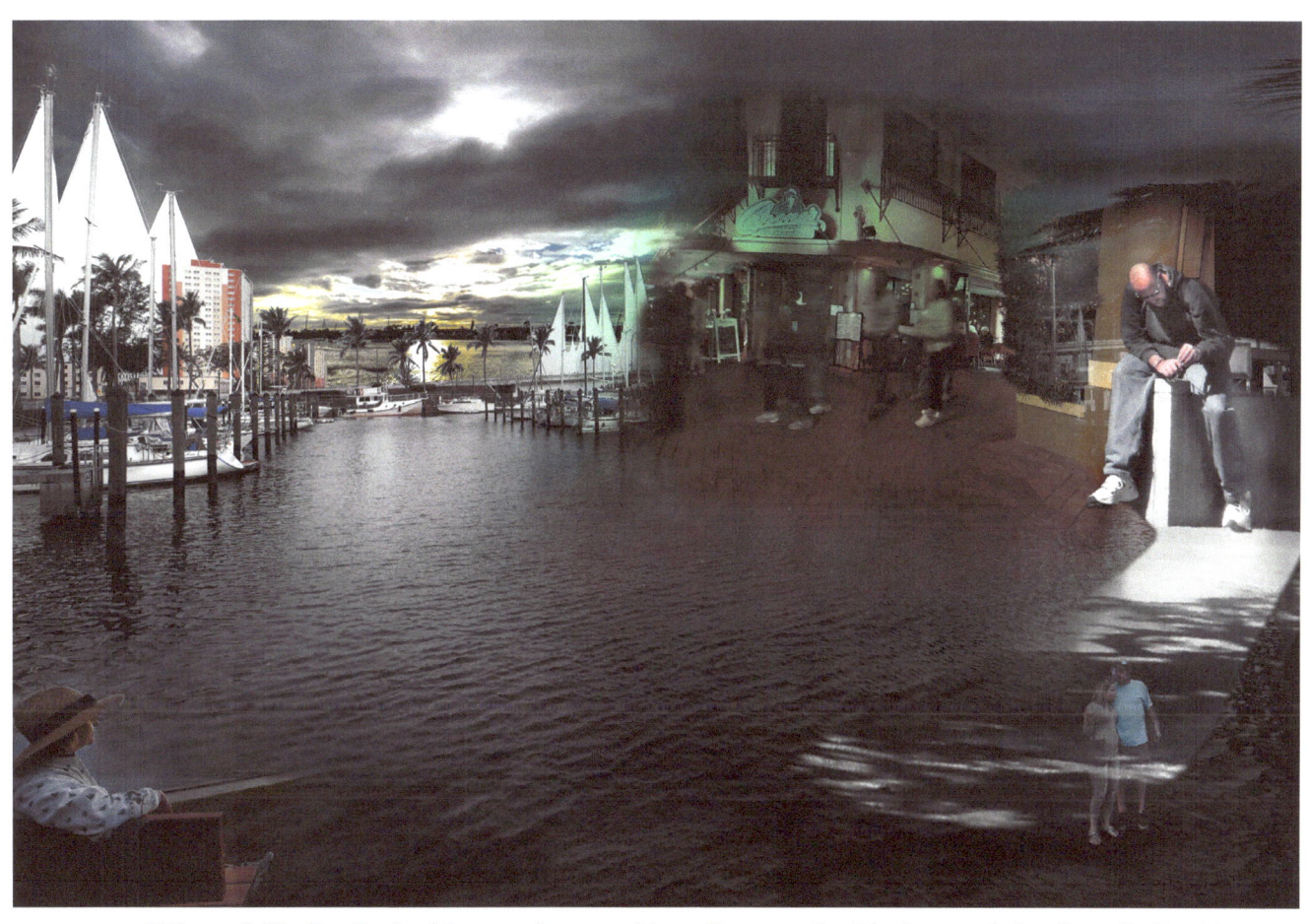

When Life Is Only Memories - *New Composite Photograph by Roy E. Rodriguez*

Have Yourself A Donald Trump White Christmas

New poem Inspired by Scott Guelcher's painting "Holidays"

Have yourself a Donald Trump White Christmas
Like you used to know,
No blacks near
And rapists back in Mexico.

Have yourself a Donald Trump White Christmas
No Obama care
In the ER
Hope you find an intern there.

Here you are as in olden days,
All white golden days of yore,
No Kwanzaa hype or Chanukah light,
Christ is back in Christmas once more.

No more fears of black and white together
Or what courts allow---
Just hang a terrorist from the highest bough
And have yourself
A Donald Trump White Christmas now.

~ Joseph Pacheco

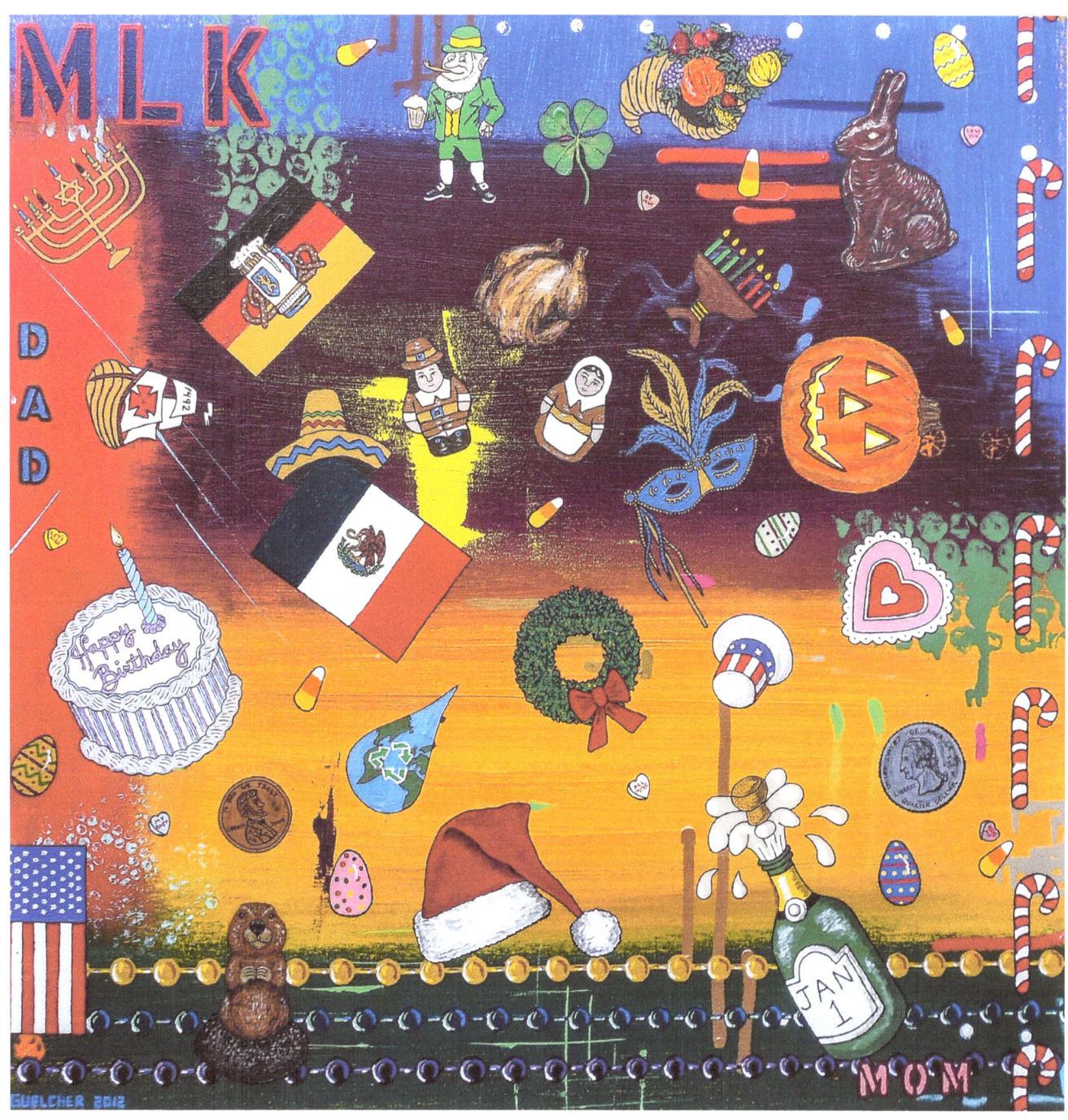

Holidays - *Painting by Scott Guelcher*

Villanelle of the Senior Tennis Round Robin

Provided Inspiration for artist William Kramer's new painting "Dust and Clay"

Returning each morning to dust and clay
We brave the ibuprophened shore
To beat oblivion one more day.

On court number one we start the fray
Not waiting for Time to settle the score,
Returning each morning to dust and clay.

Life's easy volleys all put away,
Above the waist-high net we soar
To beat oblivion one more day.

We spin and slice to dupe our prey
With chips and drops and lobs galore,
Returning each morning to dust and clay;

No ace or smash to ease our way,
But rallies longer than ever before
To beat oblivion one more day.

So toward the final court we'll play
Tomorrow and forevermore,
Returning each morning to dust and clay
To beat oblivion one more day.

~ Joseph Pacheco

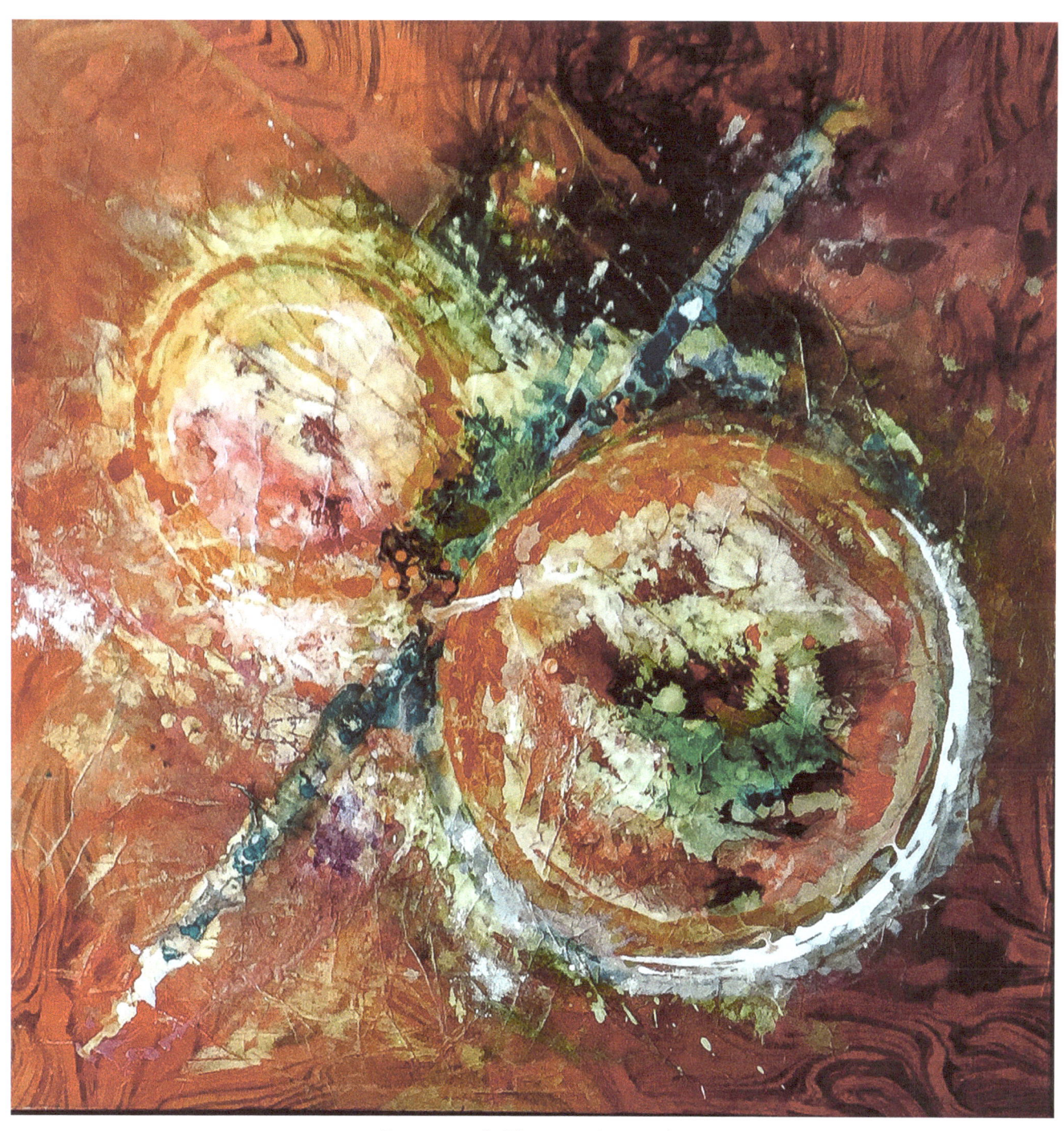

Dust and Clay - *New Abstract Painting by William Kramer*

Down The Rabbit Hole

New Poem Inspired by Kenneth A. Vinton's painting "Down the Rabbit Hole"

The layers upon layers of brilliant light led Mitch Gilbert
down the rabbit hole.   He knew there would be zones of despair,
but maybe auras of genuine happiness and joy down there, too.

We're not talking real rabbits. They just haunt the painting.
And it's not a burrow for dreams of baby rabbits, but one where
people face the Life they've carved, the connections we built.

Each layer has at its heart, all the things you've accomplished
plus the dusty, musty depths of every dream we've left undone.
Mitch has quit any longer pretending not to know what he knows.

Piled up in one of the layers, he faces the three jobs he quit,
just walked away, like the marriage, like the Daddy place he left
unfilled for their two sons and the wandering dropout daughter.

The ex-wife reminded him of the daughter's birthday and
the guilt she pounded out with the date. Mitch stayed out
of the bar three nights and had money to buy the kid something.

He's alone in The Rabbit Hole, no one to consult with about
what you get a 16 year old soon to be 17.   Alone, an idea came.
He didn't have to be completely a lousy Dad. He counted the money.

Went to a pet store and bought a cage, and not for a cat. Yep for a rabbit.
He would help her set it all up. A dish for water. A pan for its food. Maybe
he'd tell her about the life down a rabbit hole, but for now, she'd just get a rabbit.

~ Sidney B. Simon

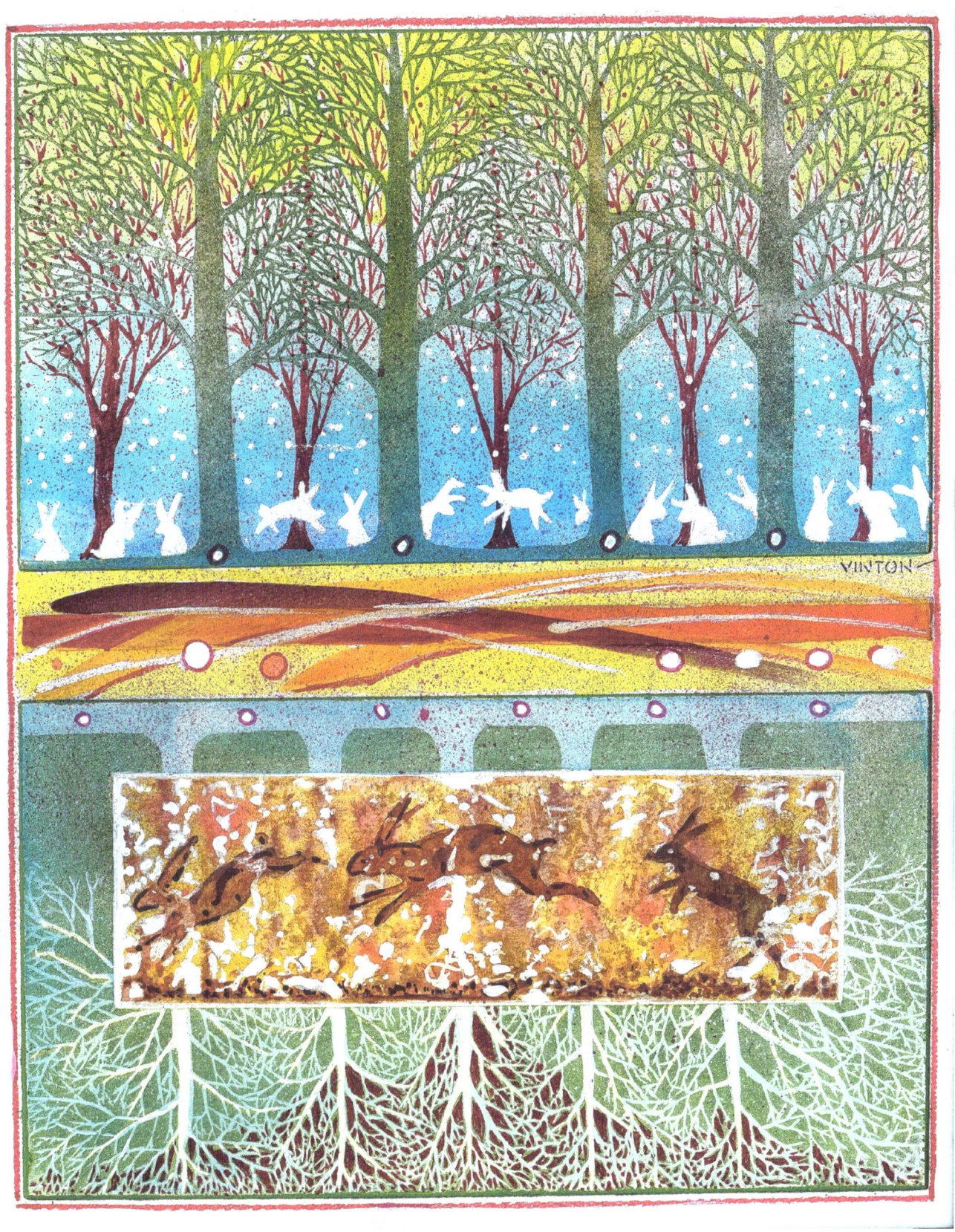

Down the Rabbit Hole - *Painting by Kenneth A. Vinton*

Monday Night Drama in Four Acts   (Dedicated to: AML)

Provided Inspiration for artist Beverly Taht's new painting "Memories"

Act I
She arrives in a flurry of excitement. Alive, eager.
Almost no other place either of us would rather be.
Maybe because she'd heard of promises of a new
camera, a reward for Montreal cell phone miracles.

Her eye is already that of a travel magazine artista.
There were two cameras to pick from. Intuitively,
she mastered both of them, and went right to work,
snapping farm silos, a mile away and flowers on table.

Act II
As the sun set, one last picture, we came in for a 35 mm. surprise.
I had found pictures, dozens of them, of her kids from long ago, moments
captured in the richness of what only her kids knew from a great mother.
No diamonds or four more cameras could have made her cry as softly.

Act III
It was time for throwing together a dinner, pitching in with wise
chopping, slicing, dicing and simmering, a perfect gourmet event.
Easy talk, of friends, of hope, lots about family, ours just having the
Annual Family Reunion, babies and teens, music, kindness and changes.

Act IV
Quick clean up, set up the couch pillows for TV, ready for the adventure.
A TV Documentary on PBS. The Rare Arc, still photographs of animals headed
for extinction around an indifferent world, captured by a genius
who has given 25 years to portraying 500 species while they are still with us.
Joel Satori. Thanks. We watched with deep admiration and stewed apple
rhubarb compote with full-fat Yogurt nestled in each other's arms, survivors.

Encore
A perfect ending for a woman who someday will be traveling and writing
about what she sees, and one day capturing a busy compote specialist in
an orchard on a day he's collecting bruised peaches, when all she really
wants is him to go with her where National Geographic sends her, forever.

~ Sidney B. Simon

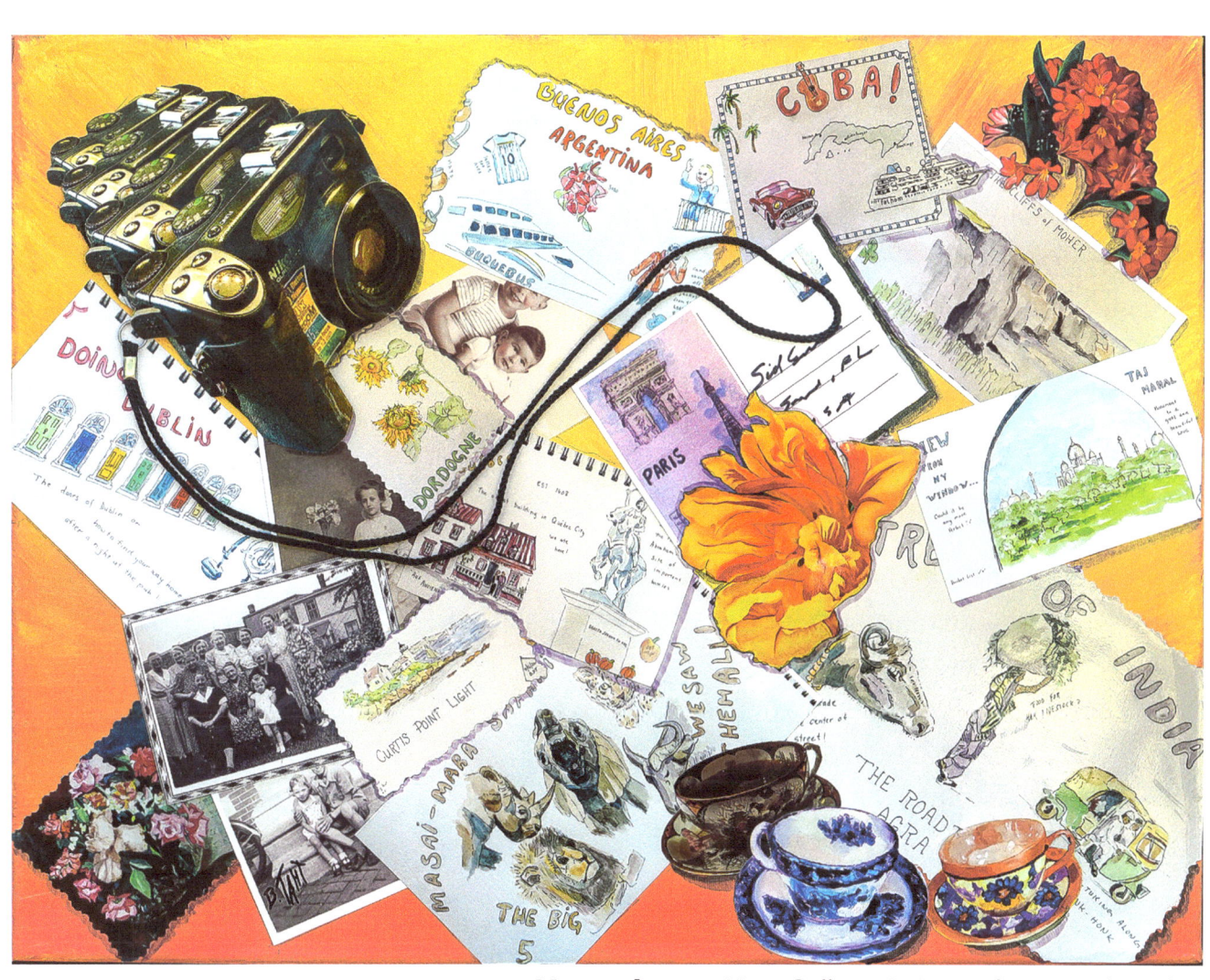

Memories - *New Collage Painting by Beverly Taht*

Barns

New Poem Inspired by Barbara Gage Mulford's painting "Northern Maine Barn"

Why do I feel longing when I pass
a weathered barn along the road?
A barn with the sweet straw smell
of summer and scarred red boards
tucked into a field where horses
graze and children climb split-rail
fences close enough to lean and
touch the horse's mane.

When I wander country roads
with nowhere special to go and
happen upon an abandoned barn,
I want to gaze awhile at the
gray patina, once dressed red,
the splintered boards, some still
hanging, and the jagged hole
in the roof that lets birds in.

Doors unlatched, one can almost
smell the animals once housed
in stalls, cats curled asleep
on sultry afternoons, and imagine
the glint of pitchforks above bales
of hay, and know a community
where neighbors came together
to build a barn.

Perhaps an abandoned barn is
a vision of the past disappearing
a little each season as it ages—
Barns slick with rain, framed in
autumn leaves or blanketed with
snow echo in the distant laughter
of children flopping on hay,
piled high after harvest.

~ Lorraine Walker Williams

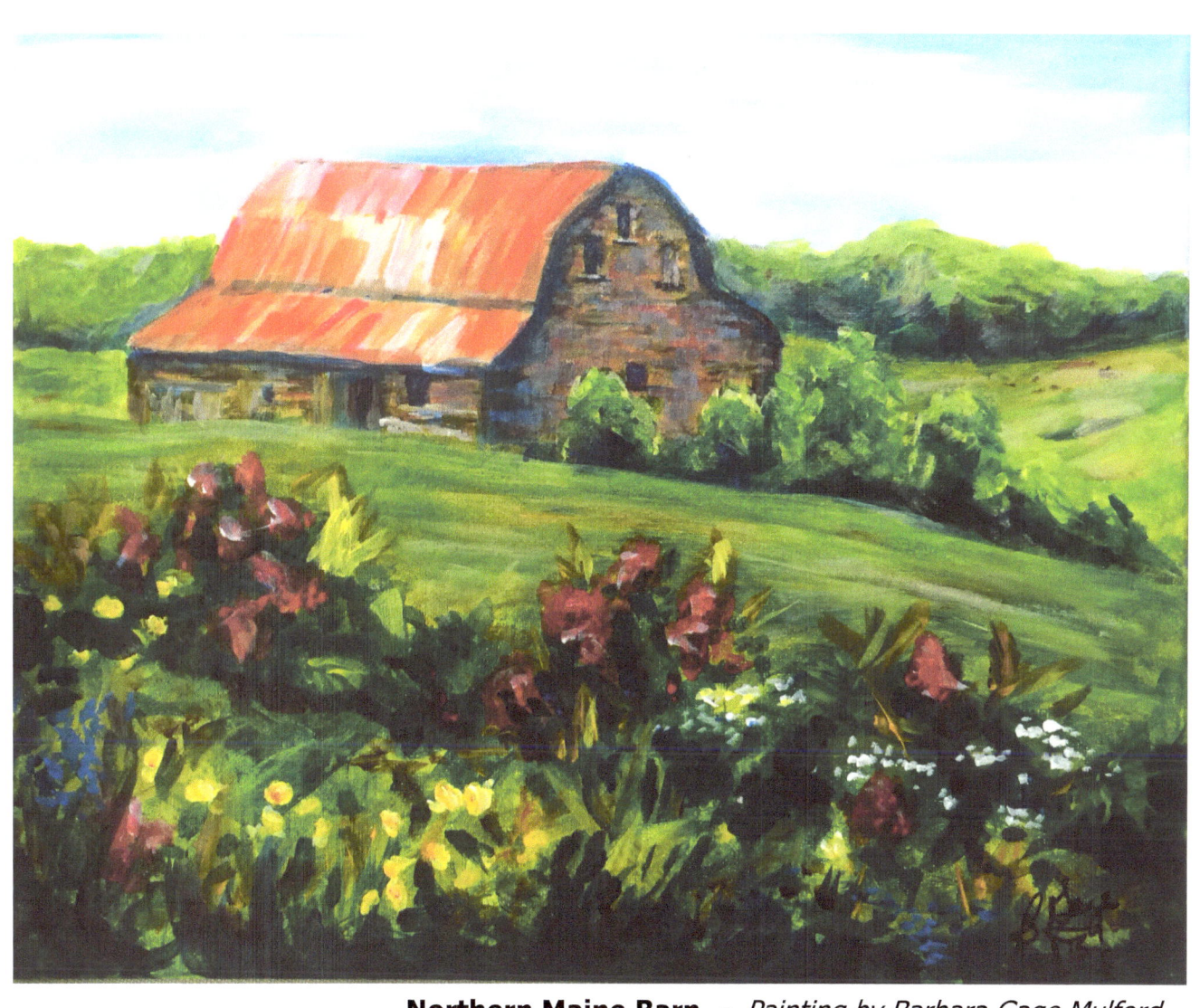

Northern Maine Barn - *Painting by Barbara Gage Mulford*

So It Was…

Provided Inspiration for artist Kenneth A. Vinton's new painting "So It Was Until It Wasn't"

So it was, until it wasn't.

    Alleged…Alleged.

Courage, risk-taking…
Women's words open Pandora's door
    a crack, a sliver of light
    strewn on the floor, on the wall—

Graffiti in shadow.

Alleged, alleged…
    Money and Power,
    enough to buy *Silence*…

Until, until…
    One voice was heard
    and one voice joined another,
    and another and another…

Speaking Truth to the mighty.

A few fell like dominoes
    were fired, removed,

said they were Sorry—
    Sorry for locking the door,
    Sorry for exposing themselves,
    Sorry for forcing themselves on another.

Some thought it funny—
    Exploiting power,
    women as objects, used and abused.

So it was, until it wasn't.
So it is, until it isn't.

    ~ Lorraine Walker Williams

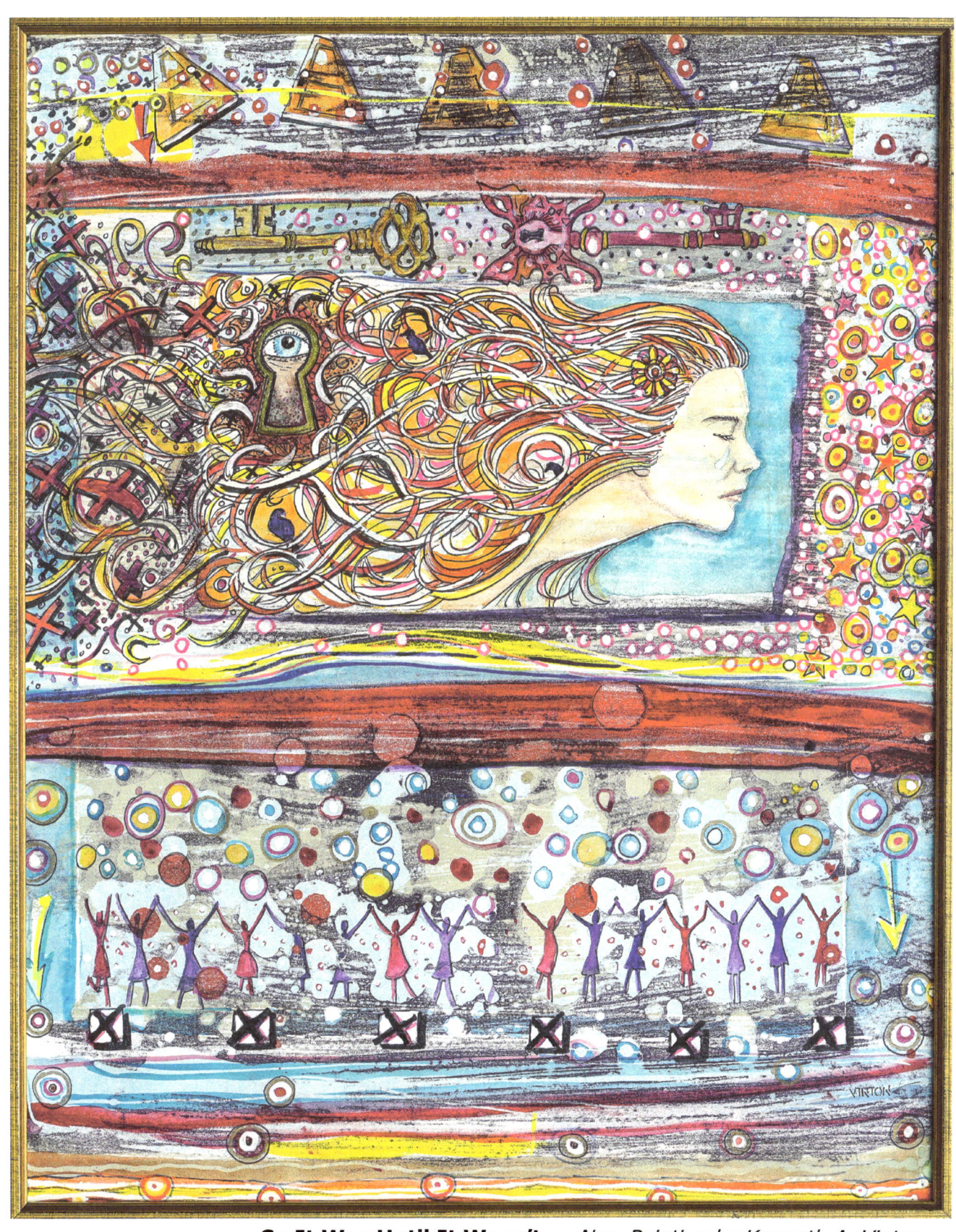

So It Was Until It Wasn't - *New Painting by Kenneth A. Vinton*

The 2018 ArtPoem Collaborators

Poet Participants:

Jamilla D. Brooks is a native of beautiful SWFL. She is a Hall of Fame MBA graduate from Florida Gulf Coast University where she currently is an Adjunct Professor. Jamilla is an Inspirational Speaker with a *Desire To Inspire* and a published author, "Beautiful You Are!: Inspired Poems." Jamilla was recently honored as one of SWFL's 40 Under 40 in the Naples Herald.

Dan England is a licensed clinical social worker, working in the mental health field, and is originally from Iowa. He is also an avid wood turner, builds furniture and enjoys kayaking.

Joyce Berrian Ferrari This is her fourth year as a poet collaborator, and her first year as a co-producer with Roy Rodriguez for ArtPoems. Joyce enjoys playing with the power of words through poetry. Working with artists is continuously a growing experience for her. Joyce resides with her husband Carl at the Jersey shore and in Fort Myers.

Chris Godwin is a Sanibel-happy wordsmith, and a participant in Island Writers and ArtPoems. A retired college administrator/professor emeritus, she's enjoying the magic of writing poetry after a career in prose: authoring textbooks, professional articles, and mountains of work-related reports. The visual arts are a particular source of inspiration. Chris's special interests continue to be the "power of story" in immigrant, women's and children's literature.

Sandy Greco finds inspiration in personal experience. A retired physician, she attended the University of Chicago, and resided in NJ before moving to Sanibel. Also a lover of music, she enjoys singing whenever possible.

Mary Beth Lundgren belongs to SWFL Poets and Gulf Coast Writers. She's authored two poetic picture books (from Clarion Books) plus a teen novel (from Henry Holt), along with many short pieces for children and adults. Born in Ohio, she's lived in Florida since 1999 with her husband, Ted, and a gorgeous black cat named Morgan.

Holly L. McEntyre is a part-time professor, an aspiring poet, and a full-time caregiver to two loved ones with dementia. This is her 3rd collaborative experience with ArtPoems.

Gary McLouth For Gary coming into what you can call poetry, creative writing or the way not to make a living, began at the knee of my grandmother who transformed the mundane into the magical, telling stories. My 4th grade teacher caught my ear with structured rhyme and rhythm, and to her occasional dismay, lost my attention during less musical subjects to the world outside the windows. Life steadily awakens around me and in me, the senses tuning experience, study and practice making art. Not much of a living, but for me, the only life worth living.

Marilyn Mecca I went "public" a few years ago and turned years of diary entries, travel notes and observations into poetry. Being retired, I enjoy my morning coffee sitting down before doing what I love to do — be an arts volunteer - at the Alliance for the Arts, at the Bob Rauschenberg Gallery and at Arts in Healthcare.

Joe Pacheco is Co-Chair of ArtPoems. Sanibel Joe's Songbook was published in 2013. Named literary Artist of the Year in 2008 by the Alliance of the Arts, he has performed his poetry in N.Y.C. and Miami, and writes a poetry column for the Sanibel Islander.

Sidney B. Simon is the author of a dozen books, mostly on Values Clarification. "Cheap Grandpa in Action" is his most recent. He is a Theater critic and MC for "Stories for Grownups." Sid was Literary Artist of the Year, 2011, almost as happy an event as being in ArtPoems right from the very first year.

Lorraine Walker Williams Creator of ArtPoems was nominated for the Pushcart Prize twice. Simply Sanibel Poems is her fifth book of poetry. Literary Artist of the Year 2009, her weekly, Poetry Place column appears at Santivachronicle.com lorrainewalkerwilliams.com.

Artist Participants:

Paul David Adamick is a retired elementary art teacher of 41 years. He now teaches drawing and painting at The Cape Coral Arts Studio. He also takes fused glass and raku clay classes at this site.

Honey Costa I always feel ready for a new art challenge. This year's subject matter was just that. In this depiction I attempt to represent my imagination and love of animals, even prehistoric. I continue to challenge myself with other techniques, compositions and subject matter. Art is my raison d'etre.

Scott Guelcher His unique style of art has become well known in S.W. Florida. This blend of Pop Art Images and abstract backgrounds has attracted galleries to frequently display his artwork. He graduated from FGCU in 2005 and received local and international recognition for his artwork. He currently teaches art at Island Coast H.S. and was commissioned to create two public art pieces at FGCU.

William Kramer I have no formal art education ... what I do have is the skill and talent provided to me naturally by the Universe. I have always worked in the field of visual arts; floral design, interior design, landscape design, and retail display. My life philosophy is based on recognizing the Universal-Energy around us and paying it forward. My abstract style is a direct representation of this philosophy.

Claude Lyles University of Missouri degree in art. Retired commercial banker. Owner of Estudio Cielo Azul. Member of Art League of Ft. Myers, Visual Arts Center Bonita Springs, Punta Gorda Arts Center, and Alliance for The Arts, in addition to ArtPoems.

Lawrence Massing A lifetime of photography has led to a degree in photography from Southern Illinois University (1973) advertising/illustration studio photography, freelance photography, and fine art photography with an emphasis on man altered landscapes and cityscapes.

Lesley Morrow is an artist whose paintings are bold, raw and sensitive to the eye. She expresses the feminine experience, the mystique, through contemporary portraiture capturing not only the strength she sees in these women and their faces but also the chaos behind the façade.

Barbara Gage Mulford A Southwest Florida resident Barbara is inspired by nature, history and current events as she creates acrylic, watercolor and oil paintings. Barbara also teaches drawing and painting at several locations. Look for her signature: B Gage.

Roy E. Rodriguez As a photographic artist, I am always interested in the process of discovery, of finding a potential image with power to grasp my attention. One may say this involves providence or coincidence, both passive actions. However, I include another element, the action of "seeing", which is active and receptive. I speak of being present in the moment of taking the photograph.

Beverly Taht As an artist, I am inspired by the grace, beauty, and power of nature and the unexpected delights of travel to new places. To capture these in an art piece is a challenge.

Kenneth A. Vinton I was born the same day Abraham Lincoln was shot, the Titanic was struck by an ice cube, and Pete Rose was born, and somehow still persevered. (Art saved me from mathematics :)   I've been a teacher, an author, an illustrator, a contractor, an accountant, a racquetball pro, an antique shop owner, a restorer of antiques, a dad, a grandpa, a docent, but always an artist. I always look forward to the next day.

Buck Ward I try to find the bits of beauty, the natural interstices in the urban coastal landscape. To find art among the myriad signs, poles, wires and parking lots, to find a beach not crowded with people, a horizon with no cell tower – that is my challenge. I try to use the light, the sky and clouds, the water, to enhance the built environment, to reveal the art of nature in the mundane works of humans.

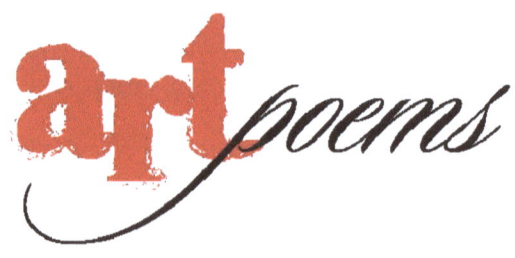

ArtPoems was created by Lorraine Walker Williams and Joe Pacheco in 2007.

Meeting at the Sanibel Public Library, they used works of art in library volumes to inspire new poetry. From this modest beginning they established ArtPoems to provide a platform for the creation of new art and poetry by collaborating artists and poets.

Since that time Lorraine, as ArtPoems Chair, with the help of Joe as Co-Chair and Larry Stiles as Treasurer, has successfully produced eleven seasons of creative inspirations.

During that period there have been nearly two hundred collaborations of artist and poet, with each collaboration producing a new work of art and poetry.

~

Each fall a group of artists and poets gets together.
They pair up by drawing names from a hat and exchange works.
The artists create pieces inspired by a poem;
the poets compose poems inspired by a work of art.
The result is a unique interchange of inspiration
through visuals and words:
ArtPoems

All works created through ArtPoems are available for sale.
ArtPoems, Inc. is a 501(c)(3) Florida not-for-profit corporation.
www.artpoems.org

www.ingramcontent.com/pod-product-compliance
Lightning Source LLC
Chambersburg PA
CBHW051217220526
45473CB00003B/1072